SPIES IN THE DEER WOODS

How to Hunt Game and Monitor Wildlife
with a Scouting Camera

Dick Scorzafava

and

Walt Larsen

STACKPOLE BOOKS

Copyright © 2008 by Stackpole Books

Published by

STACKPOLE BOOKS
5067 Ritter Road
Mechanicsburg, PA 17055
www.stackpolebooks.com

Printed in China

First edition

10 9 8 7 6 5 4 3 2 1

Cover design by Wendy A. Reynolds
Cover photograph by Walt Larsen

Library of Congress Cataloging-in-Publication Data

Scorzafava, Dick.
    Spies in the deer woods : how to hunt game and monitor wildlife with a scouting camera / Dick Scorzafava and Walt Larsen. — 1st ed.
        p. cm.
      ISBN-13: 978-0-8117-3512-4
      ISBN-10: 0-8117-3512-5
  1. Deer hunting. 2. Scouting cameras. I. Larsen, Walt. II. Title.

SK301.S273 2008
799.2'7652—dc22

                                                            2007046773

Contents

Foreword

Some of the best books never written are dreamed up—and eventually forsaken—by skilled hunters who have incredible insights about deer, bear, elk, and other wildlife, but have neither the time nor the interest to sit down and share their expertise with the rest of us. Then again, it is also rare to find skilled writers whose hunting insights are worth publishing. And rarer yet is to find two such communicators, willing to team up and share their specific hunting knowledge with any and all who ask. Most such endeavors usually fail because of egos, selfishness, and other petty flaws that can mar the personalities of talented people.

Therefore, the book you are holding is unique. If someone were to assign a book project on scouting cameras, and request the best tactics and setups for using them, Walt Larsen of Minnesota and Dick Scorzafava of Massachusetts would top the list of potential authors. Although they developed their hunting and scouting camera expertise independently from each other, they have helped one another communicate their insights and tactics through DVDs, television, and magazines.

This book culminates those many years of teamwork, allowing Walt and Dick to brainstorm and mesh their considerable talents to create one impressive, comprehensive package. Perhaps just as importantly, they did it without ruining a good friendship.

One of the first venues to tap into this team's expertise was *Deer & Deer Hunting* magazine. I met both men while serving as the magazine's editor, and remember marveling at the hundreds of real-world photos Walt Larsen produced in the mid-1990s through his work with early scouting cameras at Scales Advertising in St. Paul. It took me a while to see the obvious, but one day in late 1999 I called Walt and said something like: "We can't stop looking at your scouting-camera advertisements. The photos you find are incredible. Could you do a column that uses those photos to give our readers insights into deer behavior?"

That conversation led to the column "Candid Whitetails," which first appeared in the June 2000 issue of *D&DH*. Readership surveys soon confirmed our belief that we had a winner. If anyone is keeping score, Dick's byline appeared in a *Deer & Deer Hunting* publication about nine months before "Candid Whitetails" began. That's when *Deer & Deer Hunting* published his feature article on decoying bucks in the 1999 Mathews Solo Cam Bowhunting annual magazine. Before long, Dick's work began appearing regularly in *D&DH* itself.

After I moved on to other publishing work, Dick helped out enthusiasts regularly with some of his most practical and insightful work yet. By then lots of people were writing about scouting cameras, but Dick's efforts stood apart. He not only understood when and where to put his cameras, but also how to set them up to capture the best action every time the shutter snapped. But as happens so often with space-crunched magazines, Dick could only introduce fellow hunters to the broader details of deploying scouting cameras to monitor the whitetail's scrapes, rubs, and feeding areas. In fact, even a three-part series might have left readers feeling cheated, and thirsting for more.

Maybe that is another good reason to publish books. They provide the space and uncluttered format to best explore the new worlds revealed by scouting cameras, and to pass along tips and advice to help others uncover the secrets of their wild places. As you read this book, you will be struck by how much we missed before scouting cameras came along, especially the images taken at night. Suddenly we could see the 10-point buck that shredded tree trunks ten inches in diameter, and wonder if he would ever reveal himself in daylight. Or maybe we finally saw that 650-pound black bear that tossed logs like toothpicks and left paw prints that made us gulp. And gulp twice more.

In many ways, scouting cameras fill in those big blank spots once reserved for our imagination. I'm sure some people would say that's not a good thing, but photos shared in the pages that follow argue otherwise.

With any luck, Walt and Dick will continue to work together in the years ahead, and this book will mark the beginning of a collaborative series worthy of every hunter's library.

Patrick Durkin
Waupaca, Wisconsin

Acknowledgments

I sincerely believe that the knowledge you gain from this book may change your hunting life forever. Everyone who reads these pages can, given the proper mindset and effort, become a much better hunter.

I consider the acknowledgments the most important part of this book. I attribute very little of my success over the years to myself because without the people around me I wouldn't have the ability to do what I love to do.

I want to thank Walt Larsen, my co-author, for helping me along the path that has led me to this high point in my career. Walt, you have been an enormous spiritual and professional mentor as well as a great friend. Working as a team for many years, we have developed a strong bond that has spawned a special relationship rarely exhibited in the hunting industry.

I am very deeply grateful to Jimmy McDonough, game biologist and deer project leader, whose loving guidance, skill, patience, and tireless efforts over the years helped me to develop into the hunter I am today. This wonderful man was never too busy for me or above sharing his knowledge with me, even when I was just a young kid.

A special thanks goes out to my friend Pat Durkin, who wrote the foreword for this book. And thanks to Mark Cuddeback from Non-Typical, Inc. who manufactures the best scouting cameras in the industry. Both have given me years of support and guidance.

I owe much to the support of others who provided me with information, materials, advice, and examples, including William McKinley, Program Biologist from Mississippi, and Jason Snavely from Drop-Tine Consultants in Pennsylvania. Both of these men did extensive research in the field using scouting cameras as a management tool for whitetail deer across North America.

Last, but not least, I want to thank all the friends and family who have supported me though my many years of scouting and hunting and who somehow, in some way, contributed to the writing of this book.

Dick Scorzafava

First I would like to thank Dick Scorzafava for his friendship and for being the model co-author. This is my first book, and Dick made it easy.

Next, I'd like to acknowledge the hours upon hours that I was author first and husband second. Thank you to Michele, my wife, for her support and understanding.

Pat Durkin, who authored the foreword for this book, was the first one who really recognized the entertainment value of scouting camera photos. It was Pat's idea for me to write my "Candid Whitetails" column in *Deer & Deer Hunting* magazine.

Finally, Mark Cuddeback is not only a valued client but also a great friend. Mark graciously offered the photos from his company's scouting camera photo contest to illustrate this book. Mark also offered his vast knowledge and expertise.

Walt Larsen

Introduction

Dick Scorzafava hails from Massachusetts where, as a young man, he grew up next door to a state biologist who took him under his wing. While still a teenager Dick was crawling into bear dens to tag sleeping bruins. By the time he was in his twenties, Dick was a well-known bear hunting guide, seminar speaker, and outdoor writer in the Northeast—a combination, sans the guiding, he has continued throughout his career. I, meanwhile, combined an expertise in marketing strategy with my passion for hunting. My advertising agency, Scales Advertising, specializes in the hunting market and represents some of the more notable names in the industry including Cuddeback, the leading digital scouting camera. Dick and I first met in the mid-1990s. Dick was a pro-staffer for one of my clients. We became fast friends and have, on numerous occasions, fished and hunted together. Today, Dick is a pro-staffer for most of my clients and a nationally recognized outdoor writer. It was this notoriety that led to Dick and Stackpole Books getting together on his first two books, *Radical Bowhunter* and *Radical Bear Hunter*. Dick and I suggested to Stackpole, given the meteoric growth in the popularity of scouting cameras, that a book on scouting cameras was in order. You are holding the result of that suggestion.

Since Dick is so adept at writing technically about hunting products, we decided that he would handle Part I, which deals with the scouting camera and how it works. Likewise, Part III discusses using scouting cameras as tools for deer management. He also wrote the scrape portion of chapter 7, and given his bear hunting expertise, the bear portion of chapter 15. Since I have been involved with scouting cameras since 1995 and have orchestrated several scouting camera contests, I took Part II, regarding hunting with scouting cameras, Part IV, which addresses other uses for your scouting camera, and the final chapter on the future of scouting cameras.

If you already use scouting cameras you, no doubt, can appreciate why both Dick and I thought this book had to be written. Scouting cameras are both a valuable tool and a wonderful toy for the deer hunter. If you have not yet purchased your first scouting camera, we hope this book encourages you to do so. You will be very glad you did, for scouting cameras open up a whole new world to the deer hunter.

Good luck and good hunting!
Walt Larsen

CHAPTER 1

How a Scouting Camera Can Make You a Better Hunter

In the last decade, the use of a scouting camera has grown exponentially as an aid to the deer hunter, which is a testament to two things: it's fun and it gives the hunter an edge. First of all, using a scouting camera is a blast. It is fun to see what the camera's eye has captured while you were not there. Everyone loves a surprise. Many deer hunters have discovered that scouting cameras give them yet another new and innovative method of hunting the elusive whitetail deer. Second, scouting cameras enhance the whole hunting experience. Remote photos provide a series of clues as to the habits and whereabouts of various deer in a certain hunting area. For the hunter who employs these photos of actual sightings, a lot of guesswork is eliminated in an effort to successfully harvest a deer, perhaps even the trophy buck of his dreams.

Back in the mid-1990s, a friend of mine who was the president of a large private hunting club in the Berkshire Mountains of Massachusetts came to me for some advice. He knew I had been using scouting cameras for a few years as an aid to my scouting program, and had been having success on quality animals during the bowhunting season. It seemed that several members, including my buddy, needed help to reveal the movement patterns of the mysterious monster bucks they thought were operating in a totally nocturnal mode. They assumed these big bucks were roaming the property under the cover of darkness because they had not been sighted during daylight hours.

I devised a program to evaluate the property by strategically locating several scouting cameras in places where the terrain would force the deer through a certain area or on trails outside of a thick swamp. Others were posted to photograph action in bedding areas. The scouting camera program lasted just over an entire year. This way all seasons were captured and the cameras were moved to different locations throughout the entire property. The results? I never got pictures of these monster bucks they believed were roaming their hunting club in the darkness of the night. I did however get many pictures of the same does, spikes, and small basket bucks on the property. After retrieving many rolls of

11/14/06   1:41 AM

Seeing is believing. Scouting cameras show you what deer are on your property and whether they are big or small.

film from my cameras and having the film developed over that year's time I came to realize that there simply were not all the mythical nocturnal monster bucks they thought were wandering the property of their hunting club.

A meeting with the members was set up to give a slide presentation of the findings. When this took place, several members commented that something must have been wrong. They felt sure there had to be some monster bucks roaming their property in the darkness of the night. After all, many of the members had seen the signs: big tracks in the snow, scrapes, and rubs. They felt there just had to be some big bucks in there somewhere on the property.

If there were any big bucks on the property we would have captured them on film, especially after such a comprehensive and lengthy use of the scouting cameras. The scouting cameras were located in many different areas and they were on duty 24/7. They were not seeing those monster bucks on the club's property because, quite simply, they were not there. If you want to kill big bucks you must hunt where big bucks exist, and the higher the numbers a certain property contains, the better your chances will be of getting an opportunity to harvest one. The photos were all the proof I needed to convince the membership that the problem was not monster nocturnal bucks on the property. What they needed was a good deer management program.

The club immediately implemented a quality deer management program on the property to correct their problem. After several years of extensive deer management on the property they started to consistently harvest several quality trophy class animals every season. We all learned valuable lessons from using scouting cameras on the property. Scouting cameras couldn't find big bucks that were just not there. But they did a great job of letting us know what *was* actually wandering the woodlands within the boundaries of the club's property. And this information brought about a new program designed to make better use of the land and to cultivate a better deer population. Instead of operating with a fantasy set of beliefs based on non-existent bucks, the factual information led the group to rethink their options and create opportunities in a proactive way, instead of just attributing lack of sightings to the nocturnal proclivities of mythical monster bucks.

The deer hunter has a definite advantage with the digital scouting camera technology that is available today. This technology has made it increasingly easier to snap a picture of the deer that are roaming around any property. Back when I started using those first-generation 35 mm film scouting cameras, they were an excellent aid in my remote scouting plan for the season. They really served me well, but the capabilities of the new digital camera models have jumped light-years ahead of the 35 mm film models. The key to switching over to digital was how nice it was to experiment with the digital scouting camera unit. I could take all kinds of test pictures to ensure that my setup was perfect and simply delete them right there on the spot. With my old 35 mm film scouting cameras I was continually wasting expensive film and running back and forth getting film processed at an additional cost. The savings on film and developing alone went well into the hundreds of dollars, not counting the fuel and time running to the local store to purchase and process film.

Let's take a look at what you can do with scouting cameras and how they can make you a better deer hunter or manager on a certain parcel of property.

PATTERN OVERALL DEER MOVEMENT

Patterning the overall deer movement on a parcel of property will allow the deer hunter to study how the deer are using the property. This information will pinpoint where and when deer are sighted at particular areas within the property boundaries. Deer don't always behave the way one thinks. A scouting camera will quickly show the "wheres" and "whens" of deer movement.

PATTERN AN INDIVIDUAL BUCK

By patterning an individual buck, the hunter may then be fortunate enough to learn that a trophy buck is within the boundaries of the property he is hunting. The scouting camera will help him find the best location to set up an ambush site. Scouting cameras can act as a great motivational tool when the hours on stand can start to wear on the hunter. Once the hunter captures a trophy class buck on film it's almost as good as actually shooting one with a bow or gun. An actual documented sighting will be a great inspirational tool for any deer hunter

There is nothing like a photo of a big buck to inspire a hunter to stay on stand.

Cuddeback Digital Camera 10/29/05 3:33 AM BubbaBrandt

to stick it out, even under the worst of conditions. When the hunter knows for certain that the area has a great buck, he will have a better attitude and a lot more perseverance in waiting it out for that trophy animal.

ELIMINATE GUESSWORK
A scouting camera can take the guesswork out of the equation that determines what is actually out there on the property. The scouting camera will tell the hunter about the quantity and quality of the deer on the property, whether good or bad. The hunter will learn if he should wait it out for the big bruiser. On the other hand, he may learn that his area does not support the quality bucks he expected. In that case, the deer hunter can decide to hunt elsewhere, or elect to lower his expectations as a quick fix for the current season. He may decide to implement a deer management program that will be a long-term investment for future seasons.The hunter will have a good indication for the buck-to-doe ratio and the age structure of the bucks. If desired, the user can perform a more formal survey that actually determines, to a very high degree of accuracy, the precise deer numbers per square mile on a property.

ANALYZE AND CREATE
Scouting cameras are excellent tools for a wildlife biologist to study deer behavior. Biologists around the globe have learned that by using scouting cameras they are able to determine how animals live and what they are actually doing at any time during the year. Images of individuals captured provide factual data.

This photo won the 2006 Cuddeback Photo Contest.

The hunter can have year-round fun using a scouting camera. It can even be a family affair involving youngsters, to get them introduced to the great outdoors. Just being able to capture nature with a scouting camera is very enjoyable; best of all, you can share the results of your efforts with everyone. Deer hunters may wish to keep their hot spot a total secret. Scouting camera photo contests are appearing all over, and anyone with a scouting camera has a chance to win because most contests will look for an interesting overall image in addition to a large-racked buck.

There are many things a scouting camera can be used for other than just hunting. They can be used for surveillance, general wildlife photography, and random image capturing at a family gathering or party. In fact, most scouting camera owners are using their units all year long. Thanks to modern digital camera technology, it hardly costs a thing to operate a scouting camera after the initial purchase of the unit.

SAVE TIME

All the accomplished deer hunters I know will agree that a victorious hunt begins with hours of scouting and preparation. In the hustle and bustle of today's society, it is difficult for the average deer hunter to find time to observe and learn the habits of the local deer. The digital scouting camera can do this for you. A scouting camera can play a huge role in how the deer hunter actually hunts an animal. All of the individuals who take their deer hunting seriously view these cameras as a standard piece of equipment that is almost as important as their bow or gun, not as technological excess.

BUILD SELF-CONFIDENCE

A digital scouting camera will make better deer hunters, because it will show where and when the movement occurs on a hunting property. This information will allow the deer hunter to set up an ambush strategy. It will not, however, give the deer hunter any kind of unreasonable high-tech benefit that will practically guarantee victory in the field. The one thing that remains a fact is that the deer hunter's self-assurance will take a huge upward turn once he is aware that roaming the woods of his property is a trophy buck. The hunter will go into the deer woods with a much deeper understanding of the buck's movement patterns. Guesses and theories will disappear and confidence will rocket as the hunter plans a hunt based on factual sightings. Just remember, finding a trophy class whitetail buck is not the challenge. Putting that buck on the ground is the proof of the pudding.

CHAPTER 2

The Inside Scoop on Scouting Cameras

Scouting cameras are, in essence, the combination of two common products: a digital or film camera and a heat-in-motion sensor. When the two are combined together into a single unit the finished product will allow the deer hunter to scout any area twenty-four hours a day, seven days a week, rain or shine. Any deer hunter looking to bag that trophy buck of a lifetime can greatly benefit from utilizing a scouting camera in his bag of tricks.

It takes more than skill and know-how to harvest good bucks consistently. It requires countless hours of scouting and revisiting deer stands and hunting an area in order to come up with a plan of attack to ambush any big buck. This need for hours of scouting poses an enormous disadvantage to hunters, because the more they trample around any hunting area the more it decreases their opportunity of even seeing a trophy buck from the area. If deer hunters truly want to see plenty of deer and especially an old mossy-horned buck from the stand, they must, in the pre-season, thoroughly scout the entire area without disturbing the deer or the hunting area. The average deer hunter just does not have the time required to do the amount of scouting that is necessary to put himself on a good buck. Daily jobs, chores, and the general demands of family and maintaining a home do not leave much free time, and the amount of annual vacation from work is minimal in terms of scouting time. A hunter would have to be a magician or have a clone to harvest a good buck once every five years—never mind every year. The good news is that, with the proper use of a digital or film scouting camera, all deer hunters can truly get the job done, and turn the odds in their favor on a trophy whitetail buck with minimal time spent scouting a given area. If there truly is a good buck on the property he is hunting, the scouting camera will take that mystery out of the equation for the hunter. The deer hunter will be able to set up an ambush plan that is backed up with factual data.

THE BASIC SCOUTING CAMERA

Broken down into its simplest components, a scouting camera is just a PIR (passive infrared) sensor and either a film or digital camera. The 35 mm film cameras that were used in scouting cameras have pretty much been made obsolete by the digital camera. Because of that fact we will only discuss the use of digital units within the scouting cameras.

Many manufacturers and marketing firms that promote digital scouting cameras refer to a PIR sensor as a "motion/heat" sensor, or a "heat-in-motion" sensor. More accurately, a PIR actually senses changes in infrared light. There are two things that will cause infrared light to change: an object either changes temperature or moves so that a new object is "seen" by the sensor. Technical jargon may not seem important to the deer hunter, but it is important to the engineer who has to design the sensors. If the engineer is not careful, his sensor will detect falling leaves and moving tree branches. The better scouting cameras on the market today have carefully designed and calibrated sensors so that the PIR only picks up the intended targets. Designing a sensor that works properly seems to be a trick only a few of the best manufacturers have seemed to master.

The design of the camera itself can represent challenges for the scouting camera manufacturer. Some companies will use an off-the-shelf, point-and-shoot camera to keep the costs of the unit down, but this causes several issues down the road for the deer hunter using the units. Unlike the point-and-shoot models, scouting cameras have four unique essentials that are as important in all better cameras. These four things—trigger time, flash performance, battery life, and housing—are critical to the performance of your scouting camera in the field.

Trigger Time

Consider a whitetail deer walking through an open hardwood area. It appears to be moving very slowly. The fact of the matter is that many times a whitetail may be covering as much as ten feet per second. This means that if the camera does not trigger almost instantly after detecting the deer, it will move beyond the camera's visibility range when the camera finally triggers. The end result will be a picture of the aft end of a deer or trees and absolutely no sign that a deer walked past the camera.

It may seem like just a simple matter to take a picture quickly, but the technology needed to do so is complex. A digital camera is essentially a little computer, and like a computer, it takes time to get started. It also needs to determine how to shoot the image in front of the lens to compensate for the variations in light levels. This is an enormous challenge and very few of the scouting camera manufacturers have figured out how to implement the proper trigger time into the unit. Many cameras require two, three, or even ten seconds to trigger, and the end result is an obviously blank picture. However, in some situations this trigger delay is not really that critical. If the hunter uses a camera exclusively on a bait

Trigger time is an essential feature in a scouting camera if you want to capture moving deer.

A slower-triggering scouting camera will result in photos of the aft end of the deer or no deer at all.

site (if it is legal where he hunts) where the deer hangs around for long periods of time, the trigger delay will still result in pictures of the deer. On the other hand, if the deer hunter plans to use the scouting camera to pattern deer on trails, he will need a camera within the unit that has a trigger time of less than one second.

Flash Performance

The PIR sensor on a scouting camera can easily sense deer out to fifty feet or even more. To capture a quality picture of these deer at night, the scouting camera will need a powerful flash. Some of the less-expensive cameras have a small flash bulb with a very limited range, some as short as fifteen feet. This may not be a serious

Cuddeback Digital Camera 11/03/06 5:22 AM   Non Typical, Inc

A long flash range enables you to see even distant deer.

problem, but deer hunters should be aware of this when they make a purchase decision. The best units out there use better cameras with a larger flash to really reach out to that deer that appears a little farther out than anticipated.

Battery Life

Many of the consumers out there today don't take battery life of a product too seriously when they are purchasing electronic equipment. Some would rather spend money on batteries over the life of a camera than invest in a high-quality product. However, replacing batteries when they fail is not always convenient when using a scouting camera. The batteries may fail days or even weeks before the hunter has a chance to check the camera, especially if the camera has been busy capturing photos. He may not even be aware of a less-than-optimal battery life due to storage or age considerations. The result is an extended period of time when the scouting camera is unable to perform its job of scouting the area. Less-expensive cameras not only will have very minimal battery life; they also will have serious issues when it gets extremely cold.

The better-quality camera will operate much longer on a set of batteries, allowing the camera to scout the hunter's area much longer between visits to replace the batteries, saving not only valuable time but capturing those images that may be irreplaceable. Also, more expensive scouting cameras will generally perform much better in frigid temperatures. Remember: a scouting camera with dead batteries is like not having a scouting camera at all.

Housing

Though not as important as the other three components mentioned, housing is important enough to require consideration. The housing is used both to hold the electronics and to attach the unit to a tree or other object. Nearly all manufacturers use some type of plastic for their housing, because the material is relativity inexpensive and extremely durable. One manufacturer, Cuddeback, has a steel container they call a BearSafe that their units fit right into for ultimate durability. Since these units are out in all types of weather conditions getting banged around, the housing has to stand up to abuse and be tightly sealed to keep the elements out. Most of the better scouting cameras have a rubber seal at the opening to achieve this.

The closure to the housing should be designed so it is quick, easy, and very sturdy. I like the units with a thumb screw rather than some type of snap. The snaps are usually weak, especially if they are made out of plastic, and do not hold up well under extreme conditions. Conversely, the thumb screw type of closure is quick, easy, and always reliable.

How the units are mounted to a tree should also be a consideration. Stay away from straps, bungee cords, or rope-type cords because they can get chewed by squirrels and other animals, causing the scouting camera to fall to the ground. Experience has taught me to use the units that screw to the tree because they are trouble-free after they are attached.

Several manufacturers use different camouflage patterns on their scouting cameras, while others use just earth tones in the plastic housing. This is a personal preference, and has nothing to do with how the unit functions. It only affects how the unit looks cosmetically. The camouflage units usually cost a few dollars more because the manufacturer has to pay the camouflage company a license fee.

SPECIAL FEATURES

Scouting cameras can do more than just take pictures. There is much more to a scouting camera than just a PIR sensor and a camera. Just like any other product available, once the basics are covered, higher-end scouting cameras are enhanced with several additional features. Some of these features may be important to an individual who wants all the bells and whistles on the scouting camera. Some cameras are available with all these features and several may only have a few. They include infrared imaging, video, theft-proofing, surveillance mode, and image viewing.

Infrared Imaging

The infrared camera is a new type of camera that uses an infrared-sensitive camera along with invisible infrared illuminations in place of a conventional strobe flash. These cameras are sensitive to invisible infrared light that the human eye cannot see. The reasoning behind this feature is that the visible explosion of light from a conventional camera flash may alarm a deer. The infrared flash prevents this. The trade-off is that the user will only get black-and-white images.

Some scouting camera users feel that deer can be spooked by the camera's flash.

The latest scouting cameras employ the use of infrared technology at night, which is invisible to deer and replaces traditional flash photography.

There are two styles of infrared scouting cameras: the type that will only take black-and-white images day and night, and the much more sophisticated types that take color daytime images and black-and-white night images. Of course, the buyer will have to pay more for a color infrared camera, but he will get full-color daytime images.

Video Clips

Some of the scouting cameras available allow the user to also take video clips of the game animal. Scouting camera manufacturers have varying approaches as to how the video is implemented, and include one of four ways:

- Video clips instead of a picture image.
- Video clips along with a picture image for each animal recorded.
- Video clips only during daylight hours. Most of the scouting cameras that use a strobe flash will only record video clips during the light of day.
- Video clips anytime during the day or night. This feature will typically be an infrared camera that can use its LED illuminations to record a video in the darkness of night.

Less-expensive scouting cameras will only let the user turn the video on or off. This type of scouting camera will pre-set the video length, which is typically ten to fifteen seconds. Enhanced scouting cameras, which are understandably more costly, allow the user to program the length of the video clip, anywhere from ten seconds to one minute. These enhanced units will also record a picture image with the video clip.

Theft-Proofing

Many manufacturers today take into consideration that a scouting camera is always left unattended in the woods and build in some type of theft deterrent or theft-prevention mechanism. Various theft-protection mechanisms are used by the manufacturers:

Padlocks. Securing the scouting camera to a tree can be accomplished several different ways. If the enclosure is padlocked shut it still can be removed from the tree. The camera can be padlocked to a tree with a cable, or screwed to a tree from the inside of the housing and then padlocked shut. The last is the most secure method of securing a scouting camera to a tree. One needs to ensure that the padlock cannot be cut off easily.

Software. Another method of theft-proofing is a software security system that is password-protected to prevent unauthorized use by another person. The owner's name and phone number can be programmed into the unit to allow recovery.

Most of the less-expensive scouting cameras have virtually no theft protection built into the unit except maybe the basic padlock protection. The best scouting cameras available will have many features to prevent tampering, deter theft, and help recover and identify stolen cameras.

Surveillance Mode

It may be obvious, but a scouting camera can also be used for surveillance. It can be used to watch your hunting property for trespassers. It can survey your cabin or hunting shack for would-be vandals. It can check a road for unauthorized vehicles. One can also monitor your deer stands for unauthorized use. It can also be used in entryways of a home or a spot that may be breached by a

When your scouting camera is not scouting deer you can use it as a surveillance camera to look for trespassers, vandals, or unauthorized vehicles.

possible intruder. A key point for using surveillance on a scouting camera is the advent of an infrared camera, which eliminates the telltale flash to warn intruders that their picture is being taken. When the memory card is full, most scouting cameras stop taking images. There is at least one manufacturer that has designed a surveillance mode into their units that will prevent the camera from shutting down when the card is full. The camera in these units will simply delete the oldest images to free up room for the new additional images being taken, like a loop. This helps assure the camera will not miss an intruder when it is set on the surveillance mode.

IMAGE VIEWING

One of the biggest advantages of a digital versus a 35 mm scouting camera is the ability to view the images in the field and at home. This can speed up the decision-making process as to where, when, and what you want to do with your digital scouting camera. There are many choices to select for image viewing, depending on your situation. One may work better than another. Some cameras now feature a built-in viewing display where you can view images in the field right on your camera. Other external devices may be purchased to view images in the field. Handheld viewers are now starting to appear on the market. The beauty in a handheld viewer is being able to scroll through the images that are on your card as well as an option to save images to your device. This allows your digital scouting camera to function with only one memory card. All you have to do is bring the reader home and attach it to your PC. Another great option for viewing images in the field is a compatible digital camera. The camera must support and read the same memory card that your digital scouting

Handheld viewers, like Cuddeback's CuddeView, allow you to check your scouting camera photos in the woods, on the spot.

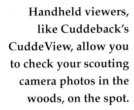

camera uses. This option works well for instant feedback, but you still need to take your card home to save the pictures. Other options for viewing images in the field include using a video camera or a compact TV attached to the camera. To do this, you need to make sure that you have the right cables and compatibility. Consult your owner's manual to see if it's even possible. Out of the field, it's very easy to view your images on a PC. A memory card reader may be necessary if your computer doesn't come with compatible memory card reading ports. All of your scouting camera images should go through your PC at some point. It is the best way to keep track of your images. It is possible to view your images at home with a TV; again you will need the necessary cords and cable that your television requires to do so. Viewing on the television is a great option when there are a lot of people who are interested in seeing the images. Having a big screen view gives you the chance to see things that might have been missed in the field.

The three essentials of a scouting camera—trigger, flash, and batteries—are critical to the deer hunter in the field. They will ensure that the hunter gets pictures of the deer that are using the area and when they are in those locations. The other features are enhancements that are nice to have on the unit but are not critical. It should be up to purchasers to decide what bells and whistles they want or need on their personal scouting cameras. Many times during the year while I'm giving seminars at shows around the country I get questions from fellow hunters about trying to figure out where to place a stand when the hunter has scouted in the traditional way and has seen huge tracks and signs of a large deer. By the size of the scrapes and rubs they just know he is a monster buck. How do they figure out which stand location to use? If they could have only seen him during their pre-season scouting or, even better, figure out where and when he is using a particular trail, they would be better able to kill him. The only way to absolutely know you are hunting a monster buck is to see him first. The best way I know to accomplish that task is to take his picture with a scouting camera. It's kind of like a fisherman using a fish finder on his boat. Once he knows where the fish are in the body of water he has a much better opportunity of catching fish. But, in all reality, the scouting camera is a much better tool for the deer hunter because it actually captures a picture of the animal for the hunter to review before the hunt. A scouting camera is an invaluable tool to help the deer hunter tip the odds in his favor.

CHAPTER 3
How to Buy the Right Scouting Camera for You

Like any other product, scouting cameras are available from many manufacturers. In this chapter, we'll explain how they differ and what to look for. Even if you already own a scouting camera, this information will be useful because you may find that an additional camera will further aid your hunting success.

QUESTIONS TO CONSIDER

Do your research to find out which brand and model is right for your specific needs. There are many different brands available to the consumer, and each person needs to decide which is best for his particular scouting style. What features does the camera include? Which manufacturer brand or model will allow a hunter to check the camera on his terms? If the user wants to leave the scouting camera out in the woods for a month, will the batteries in the unit go dead after only two weeks of use and miss two weeks of images?

How Much Does It Cost?

Considering price is an important factor for most people when purchasing a scouting camera. Is the lowest-priced scouting camera the best value for an individual's needs? Many of the cheaper scouting cameras have very slow trigger speeds, they tend to miss what goes by them, and you end up with a picture after the animal has passed by the lens. It is important to know what items are included with the purchase of a scouting camera, because many of those items can be expensive. Many digital scouting cameras don't come with a memory card and the film units don't come with batteries or film. If you are purchasing a film scouting camera, weigh the options of having to develop a lot of film and possibly having to pay for developing blank or black photos. Other important factors of a film camera to consider are not being able to review the photos instantly in the field, and the time plus cost it takes to go back and forth purchasing and getting the film developed. Sometimes an hour is too long to wait, and speedy service is usually obtained at a higher cost.

Do I Have to Own a Computer to View my Images?

Using a digital scouting camera is not out of the question if you don't have a computer. Many think you need both components but that is not true anymore because photo print stations are available at discount stores like Target, Wal-Mart, Walgreens, and so on. You can also get a printer that just prints photos. Also, a digital memory card reader can be purchased to view the images, or if you have a digital camera that will read the same format, you can install the card in the camera and view the images right away. A computer may help you view, store, and share your images, but it is not necessary.

Which Accessories Will I Need?

Look for compatible equipment when purchasing a scouting camera. Are there any accessories that can be purchased that will assist in your scouting plans? Does the scouting camera come with different mounting options? Are there steel enclosures available for the unit that will allow you to use the scouting camera for other animals beside deer, like bears, that could damage or even destroy the unit?

How Does the Scouting Camera Trigger?

Learn how the different scouting cameras trigger: is it by motion, heat, or a combination of both? The better scouting cameras will have two detection fields. To quote my buddy Walt Larsen, "Heat in motion makes the most sense in a scouting camera." The sensor detects changes in infrared light, which is caused by either heat or motion, so having both in the unit is much better.

Trigger speed is critical in your scouting camera, especially if you are planning to use the unit mostly on trails, because you need a much faster trigger speed on trails to catch the image of the deer before it gets out of the frame. The less-expensive cameras have much slower trigger speeds on their units, so be sure to research that before purchasing a scouting camera.

Which Manufacturers Offer the Best Customer Assistance?

Which scouting camera manufacturer offers the best training program for you? If you are a first-time buyer, learning a new technology can be difficult and very frustrating. Find out if there is a place you can go for support or help if you are having difficulty, like a web site or customer service line with a technician to answer any question that may arise. Also talk to people who have been using digital scouting cameras for a season or more. These are the people who have already gone out and made a purchase on one or more scouting cameras. Learn from them by finding out what they liked and didn't like about the unit they purchased.

Which Model Is Best for Me?

Within a specific brand name, find out which scouting camera model fits your needs best. Many of the scouting camera models have options that work in daylight, at night, with infrared, with video modes, and with night video capability. Decide which options might work best for your particular needs. Some people feel that the flash of a scouting camera when taking a picture in low light or darkness scares some deer off. With the infrared technology available today, it is possible to take a nighttime photo without setting off a bright flash.

How Much Will I Use the Camera?

When will you be using the scouting camera? Some people use them only during the fall, starting right before the season opens. Others use their scouting cameras all year long, making a fun thing out of it and involving the entire family.

How often you plan on checking the camera is important because if you have a scouting camera set up in a remote area hours from your home it will be difficult to check on it more than once per month. You may want a unit that will run on a set of batteries for at least a month.

Why Would a Hunter Need More Than One Scouting Camera?

If a hunter wants to scout different plots of land or different areas on the same property at the same time to determine which one presents the best opportunity for a good buck, he will need more than one scouting camera. It is also possible to pattern a certain animal with multiple scouting cameras strategically placed on a piece of property. I have had very good luck placing scouting cameras in both the bedding and feeding areas of a mature buck to pattern his movements.

If the deer hunter is planning on owning multiple scouting cameras in the future, it is important to consider buying the same brands, because they will have the advantages of being able to share the compatible accessories, including the cards.

Is It safe to Use a Scouting Camera on Private and Public Land?

Using a scouting camera on private land normally would not present a problem for the deer hunter. However, we have heard from at least one manufacturer that most camera thefts seem to happen on private land—not really what one would expect to hear. But, the conclusion is that when trespassers get photographed, they steal the scouting camera. On public land there are no trespassers and the camera is less likely to be stolen simply to cover a crime. Therefore, we

This photo was taken on public land. Contrary to popular belief, most scouting camera theft occurs on private land.

Most scouting camera thefts are the result of trespassers opting to remove the evidence.

recommend that private land owners who are concerned about trespassers consider a scouting camera with good theft protection. On public land we recommend a scouting camera that can be locked to a tree. In all cases, name branding and password protection are also good features to consider when theft is a concern.

MATCHING A SCOUTING CAMERA TO A HUNTER

A key step before choosing a scouting camera should be to honestly assess what type of hunter the prospective buyer is. This determination should be made well before a purchase is made. Because of the extreme performance and large price differences in scouting cameras, the hunter will greatly benefit by looking at how he will use the scouting camera. Let's take a look at some common hunter types and investigate how they would likely use a scouting camera. From this information, one can determine what features are important and which are not. This is not unlike a hunter purchasing a new rifle: first you determine how the rifle will be used, then you select the caliber, then the particular rifle model. The hunter would not be well equipped if he wanted to use a .223 caliber rifle for, say, elk or moose, nor would he want to use a .300 WSM for squirrels or rabbits. The hunter needs to choose the right gun for the job, and likewise, the right scouting camera for the job.

The Weekend Hunter

A weekend hunter is defined as the guy who only hunts a few days during the season and whose primary objective is to get out there and enjoy the outdoors. These guys typically hunt during the gun seasons, and are just looking to shoot a deer. They may dream of a trophy buck, but the only way they are going to get one is with the help of a guide or the once-in-a-lifetime lucky break.

How can the weekend hunter benefit from using a scouting camera? Once a weekend hunter starts using a scouting camera, watch out: one of two things is likely to happen. First, because these weekend hunters typically don't have refined hunting skills, they will probably not have a great deal of success capturing deer images with the scouting cameras. This may lead to frustration and the false belief that there are not many deer in their hunting area. This will lead to even less serious hunting and the weekend hunter will actually begin to hunt less because the scouting camera results have discouraged him.

However, a second scenario is more likely. Once the weekend hunter starts using a scouting camera, he will begin to capture images of deer. He will study these deer images throughout the week, and begin to look forward to setting up and checking his scouting camera for more deer images. In a very short time the hunting bug will begin to take hold, and he will begin to spend more time in the woods setting up the scouting camera, moving the unit from place to place, and suddenly, the weekend hunter will be transformed into a serious deer hunter. I have seen this transformation happen over and over again in the last several years, and it is sheer enjoyment to witness these individuals emerge. The best part is that it usually only takes a few weeks to happen. Because scouting cameras are so addictive, they will actually turn the passive deer hunter into a serious hunting machine.

The weekend hunter is like most consumers when they purchase a product. He starts out on the low end and works his way up the quality ladder as he begins to appreciate the quality and performance differences between low-cost and higher-cost products. For example, most deer hunters start out their hunting careers with a low-cost rifle with open sights. But after just a few years, they move up to a quality high-performance rifle with a scope attached. However, this logic should not be used to purchase scouting cameras. Once a person realizes the benefits of a better unit it will greatly outweigh the cost. The low-cost scouting cameras normally have too many compromises to be a great aid in the field. Spend a bit more now to avoid buying another camera next season.

Trophy Deer Hunter

Just the words "trophy hunter" have become the buzz words in our sport today. A lot of people believe they are true trophy deer hunters, but the reality is that most are just deer hunters. What really separates the true trophy hunter from the average deer hunter is not the trophy hunter's refusal to stop until he gets his trophy, but the fact that he won't settle for anything less. Many so-called trophy hunters will claim to pass up a nice 8-pointer all season, only to take that same deer the last week or day of the season. This is not a trophy hunter; this is an opportunist who has to shoot a deer every season. The true trophy hunter knows that a good buck is not good enough, and only the buck he desires is worthy of a shot.

This type of deer hunter needs a scouting camera that can do it all. He will place several cameras out on a piece of property to determine and pattern buck movement, placing units at bedding areas, feed areas (especially feeder or bait stations if legal), primary trails, and scrapes. The trophy hunter has to be able to have 100 percent accurate scouting data if he is going to be consistently successful every season. His equipment can't fail him when the time has come, and being in the right stand means having accurate scouting information from scouting equipment that is totally reliable and accurate. This means

A reliable scouting camera is crucial to the trophy deer hunter.

2/11/06 9:22 AM   Patrick Sneed   Cuddeback

no dead batteries, no missed images because of slow trigger time, and long distance flash performance.

Biologist or Property Manager
The biologist or property manager is usually deeply involved in QDM (Quality Deer Management). To accurately manage a parcel of property, bringing out its greatest potential, he needs to have accurate data to analyze what quality of deer is roaming the woods. He needs to know the age structure, the buck-to-doe ratio, and the overall health of the deer herd. That's just for starters. These individuals will go well beyond to achieve the quality of bucks desired on the property. The best way for these professionals to access the data required to accurately analyze the deer herd on any property is with scouting cameras. The scouting camera is a great tool because it provides a much more accurate account of the deer herd on any property than did previous methods. Much more precise and reliable than ever before, scouting cameras placed in key locations and at particular times of the year will provide a very accurate census of the deer herd. To achieve a high level of accuracy, and to do these surveys correctly, these professionals require top-quality equipment. Because of the sheer numbers of images that will be captured, perhaps many thousands per year, these professionals need to make sure of two things: the scouting camera must capture images of every single deer that walks past the camera's lens, and the camera must be affordable to operate. Using a scouting camera that eats batteries could end up costing hundreds of extra dollars per year out of a budget just in batteries. This money would be much better spent upfront on high-quality scouting cameras. The better-quality scouting camera will help the biologist or property manager in several areas. He will capture more images of deer by virtue of its faster trigger time, and it will prevent downtime caused by dead batteries.

Guide and Outfitter
A really good guide uses scouting cameras in very much the same way as a biologist or property manager to access the deer herd on his property. But he also has some other specific, additional needs.

If he is smart, the scouting camera's images taken of good bucks can be used to attract potential clients. Many use the images of bucks to decide which bucks to harvest and which to pass up for the next season. Also, they use scouting cameras to determine the stand placements for their clients.

The guide/outfitter needs a very reliable unit because of its continuous use, which is typically six months or more per year. He also requires a fast trigger speed to ensure that trails are covered and that they will get the image of the deer. Long battery life is critical because the guide/outfitter typically has much more work to do than time. Scouting cameras need to be checked when time permits, not when the cameras need to be checked to change batteries.

10/20/06   8:47 AM

Outfitters are using scouting camera photos like this one to attract customers.

We are partial to the higher-end scouting cameras and don't really care too much for the cheap ones, because that is just what they are—cheap. There is an old saying that you get what you pay for and that couldn't be truer when it comes to a scouting camera. The truth of the matter is that I'm a serious hunter. I use the best equipment I can afford, and sometimes a little better than I can afford. After I have been sitting in my stands for hundreds of hours over many weeks or even months of cold days, and that buck finally presents a shot, I want the best bow in my hand, the best arrow, and the best broadhead to guarantee that I won't miss because of mechanical failure. At this critical moment I do not want anything to go wrong with my equipment. So I always shoot the best I can afford. My scouting camera is no different.

The plain truth is that inexpensive scouting cameras just don't work in enough situations for me to even consider them as a serious scouting tool. They make decent novelties, perhaps, but they are certainly not the tools that will help put a record-book buck on my wall. For this, I want a scouting camera that triggers fast enough that I can use it on a trail or a scrape. I want a camera that will operate for weeks on end with the same set of batteries, whether it is sweltering hot or frigid cold. My scouting cameras are in the field all season and most of the summer. When that trophy buck shows up, I want my scouting camera to be as reliable as my shooting. It better not miss, and it takes a good scouting camera to not miss. I may not want or need all of the enhancements but I want a superior unit that offers optimal performance in the field.

CHAPTER 4

Scouting Cameras
and Your Computer

Today's digital scouting cameras give you the ability to interface with your PC and other electronic devices. This chapter will discuss how to download, organize, and store your images on your computer to make the entire scouting camera experience more informative and entertaining.

It is not entirely necessary that a person have a computer to view the images taken by a digital scouting camera. You do need to have a memory card to save and transfer the images to another viewing device. Most people like to have more than one memory card so they can swap out the card when they go to check the images on the scouting camera. If you have a digital camera that reads the same type of memory card as your scouting camera, or if you have a viewing device, you will have the ability to view the images right on the spot. A digital camera can be used for viewing images taken by the digital scouting camera and it can also be used to delete images from the memory card. The problem with a digital camera is that it does not have a good way of storing the images taken by the scouting camera, especially if the person is using the digital camera for other personal uses.

The memory card can be taken to one of the many photo printing kiosks in discount or drug stores. Just insert the memory card into the correct spot on the machine and follow the simple prompting instructions to view and print the images. You can also create a disk to store your images, leaving you free to delete those shots from your memory card. Then your memory card can be reused.

The best piece of equipment for effectively managing the digital scouting camera images is a modern personal computer. Macintoshes or PCs both work well and it's more of a user-compatibility question for the consumer on which direction to go here. The major reason a computer is the best format is that it has the capability to manage all the scouting camera information in many ways. If you save images directly to your computer, you eliminate the need to create a separate disk, unless you want to do so as a backup.

COLLECTING IMAGES

Once the scouting camera has been set up in the woods for a period of time, you need to collect the images that were captured. Give the scouting camera at least a week in the same location before checking the unit for images. If you are using a brand-new unit, make sure everything is working properly before placing it in the woods, especially if your hunting area is a distance away. Try out a new unit before using it to record images that you will need to help determine your hunting strategy. Once you are sure of the operation and performance of the unit, you can place it in your preferred location in the woods and let it capture images for a week or so before retrieving the results.

Always remember that it is critical to manage your human scent when you are setting up the scouting camera. This includes making scent-free progress along the route to and from where the scouting camera is set up. Imagine it is actually during the season and the scouting camera location is your treestand. This is especially important if you plan to keep the unit in that same location. You will literally re-pattern the deer right out of the area if you are not conscious of all the human scent you are leaving behind. (See "Human Scent Elimination" in chapter 7.) Most times when I'm going out to check a certain camera, I don't know whether or not I will be moving it to another location. It all depends on the number of images the scouting camera captures and what may have happened in the area since the last time I was there. If the scouting camera has a full card with many images of numerous sightings or an outstanding individual, the more likely it is that I will want to keep it in the same location. Once you know

8/16/06 8:13 PM

Try out your new scouting camera in the backyard to familiarize yourself with its operation.

the number of images the scouting camera has taken, it's time to remove the memory card or film from the camera. With a film camera, you would obviously replace the film with a new roll. In a digital camera, you would do the same, only this time you would use a memory card. Make sure to carefully follow the manufacturer's instructions, as all cameras can have a different process for removing the memory card. The memory card or even the camera could be damaged if the memory card is removed or replaced incorrectly.

With all the new technology available, viewing images in the field is feasible and quite easy. Companies such as Cuddeback Digital make viewers, which allow you to view and transfer images to a small handheld device. It is also possible to view images in the field using a digital camera that reads the same type of memory card. With a digital camera, you have the ability to view and delete the images, but they cannot be transferred to the digital camera itself.

When all the images on the scouting camera are collected, it is always wise to do a quick scan of the entire scouting camera, checking for battery life, any damage from animals or Mother Nature, and any other problem that may have occurred since the unit was checked last. I also like to carefully look around the entire area to see if anything has changed that would make me want to reposition the scouting camera. If I'm bear hunting I always look very closely around the bait location for big bear sign. Always make sure the scouting camera is activated before leaving the woods.

DOWNLOADING IMAGES

When the user is ready to download images onto the computer he will need some way for the computer to read what is on the memory card before the images can be transferred to the computer. Many of the newer computers come with ports that are designed to read memory cards. If your available computer doesn't have the proper-sized port, there is no need to worry. There are digital memory card readers that can be purchased and plugged right into the computer's USB port.

Plug the memory card into the port or reader and wait for the computer's instructions when it recognizes the newly found hardware. If for some reason the computer doesn't recognize that anything has been plugged in, you may have to go to the "my computer" option and then click on the desired drive and have the computer "read" or browse that drive.

The computer will be automatically formatted with a program to view images. Many cameras write the digital photos with the file extension "jpeg." By following the computer's prompts, the images should appear on the computer screen. If you are having problems on your first run-through, you may need to consult the owner's manual of the digital scouting camera or computer.

VIEWING IMAGES

The images the scouting camera took should be downloaded on the computer and up on the screen ready to view. This is where I like to take a good hard look, carefully studying each image to see the minor details the scouting camera captured that could be important. Is there a set of peering eyes in the background? Was I fortunate enough to capture something really astonishing? With a digital file I'm able to zoom right in to any area to see the finer points in the picture. Always examine each photo to see if any patterns can be identified, check carefully to see if the same deer is in multiple photos, make sure to note the times, and so on. Viewing the images on your computer can be exciting and very entertaining not only for you but also for the entire family.

DELETING IMAGES

The ability to delete an image or multiple images is one of the main selling points for the digital scouting camera category. Most of us have gotten a candid photo of ourselves addressing the camera for image retrieval or the scouting camera photo that doesn't have anything in it. It's always nice to have the ability and option to delete these duds without investing in a print. I hesitate to delete much when it comes to photos with any animal in them. Keeping photos of all fawns, bucks, and does will allow you to make better scouting assessments after time has passed. If I delete images of this year's spike buck, I will never get to see the progressive changes of that animal over time. This is good advice because the space a digital photo from a scouting camera takes up on the computer is minimal. I have a lot of avid scouting camera users who tell me I'm crazy because they get two hundred images at a time and their computers would be full of unneeded images. I must be a pack rat to keep them all. Use your best judgment and remember that once you delete the image from the file, it will not be available to view again. Period.

PRINTING IMAGES

When you have captured what you believe is the perfect photo for printing and you want to print the image to show all of your friends, there are several ways to print the image. The best way is to take the digital memory card to a place that does photo printing and have it professionally run at your desired size. These facilities use quality photographic paper and have the equipment to produce a very high-quality picture even in sizes up to 8 by 10 inches. Otherwise you can print them off at home on your computer printer using either a color or black-and-white printer. Depending upon your printer, these photos may look pixelated and lack quality, but for the most part they can provide an accurate assessment of what you are trying to show. If you plan to print lots of pictures over time, consider purchasing a color photo printer and quality photo paper.

These printers are quite reasonably priced and one would be a worthwhile investment because it could also be used to print the family photos taken with your digital camera. However, the ink and paper costs do add up quickly.

STORING IMAGES

Organization for all your hunting gear is critical during the hunting season, and the same logic applies to all the images taken with your scouting camera. Having a good system is very important in managing your scouting, so you will be able to organize an overall strategy to ambush any good bucks that were captured on the scouting camera. A computer will allow you to make as many folders as needed to organize all the images you have captured with the scouting camera during the year. Organize by date, location, on which scouting camera each image was taken, or any other category that fits your needs.

Remember to back up important images. If your computer should crash you will lose all of your images if they are only stored electronically on your hard drive. I always make a backup CD of each set of images and label it. This way I can access images and keep my computer files manageable. Some photo printing software will also allow you to print a contact sheet of all of the images, so you get a thumbnail view that you can quickly scan without opening the image files one by one.

The scouting camera is unquestionably the most effective scouting aid ever produced for the deer hunter, but most guys really don't take full advantage of all the information gathered. It is nearly impossible to determine anything from the pages and pages of information in hunting notebooks, the spots marked on a map, and all the images collected from the scouting cameras. Scouting camera software available today will allow the deer hunter to maximize his scouting efforts on the computer. This software allows the deer hunter to organize all this valuable information into a very easy-to-use program. Like putting the puzzle together, the hunter can combine field notes, map points, and images to create a complete record of deer sightings.

There are many different brands of digital scouting cameras and computers and just as many different ways to use them. It is important that you first consult your owner's manual to understand your camera's capabilities. It is also important to know your computer from working with image management or software that manages your images. Once you understand how these work, keep reading hunting literature to see what advances are made and how you can optimize your scouting camera experience. Remember to organize and mark your files as they can quickly become hard to recall. Back up images on a CD to prevent loss of your image bank in case of a computer crash.

CHAPTER 5

How to See What Is Out There

Now the fun begins. You've purchased a scouting camera (or cameras) and have familiarized yourself with its operation. The next step is to determine where to locate your scouting camera. First, you'll decide what you want to accomplish. In other words, what are your scouting camera goals? There are lots of possibilities. Most first-time scouting camera users just want to get some photos. My suggestion for you, if this is your case, is to put your scouting camera on a favorite trail, overlooking a scrape (assuming it is during the rut), or, best of all, overlooking a food source. By locating your scouting camera in a high-traffic location, you will soon gain confidence in its ability to do its scouting job.

Once you've accomplished your initial goal of just getting some good photos, you'll probably fall into one of seven different goal categories. If you are like me, you'll probably want to find a single big buck to hunt on your property. Or you'll want to do some prospecting to determine what bucks are using your property. Perhaps you will want to assess potential hunting sites. If it is during the hunting season you might want to use your scouting camera to monitor one spot while hunting another. You also might want to use your scouting camera to determine when and/or where the deer are coming into a field or food plot. Your scouting camera can also be used as a tool for assessing the deer herd on your property for management purposes. Or your scouting camera may simply be a source of recreation and you hope to get some interesting photos. Let's look at each of these different situations individually.

FINDING A BIG BUCK TO HUNT

Right or wrong, many deer hunters today are enamored with antlers. You can argue that hunting should be more about the experience than the result. But, thanks to the proliferation of magazine articles, television shows, and books that focus on trophy deer hunting as opposed to experiential deer hunting and, arguably, to our society's increasing interest in results, the fact of the matter is that we deer hunters love to hunt big bucks. Quite frankly, I believe our love for antlers, coupled with the fact that there are more big bucks to hunt today than ever before, explain the explosive popularity of scouting cameras. Everybody wants to find that big buck.

So how does one go about using a scouting camera to find a big buck? Really, using a scouting camera is just another form of hunting. This means you will use many of the same tactics to find a big buck with your scouting camera as you would while hunting with your gun or bow and arrow. However, hunting with your scouting camera has numerous advantages. First, your scouting camera does not get cold and tired. Nor does it need to eat or sleep. This means it can hunt 24/7. Second, your scouting camera can hunt at night when deer are generally more active. And third, you have the opportunity of using multiple scouting cameras at the same time.

As with hunting, your odds are better if you put your scouting camera where deer spend most of their time. And that means where deer eat or sleep. Bedding areas are generally excellent places to locate a scouting camera to find a big buck. If you have a known, frequently used bedding area on your property, by all means locate a scouting camera there. The trick is to get into the bedding area to deploy your scouting camera without disturbing the big bucks you are trying to find. Obviously, traipsing through a bedding area during the day when a big buck is likely bedded there is not a good idea. Heavy cover typically characterizes a good bedding area. This makes it easier for you to access. Trails leading to and from bedding areas are optimal locations for your scouting camera. So carefully access the perimeter of one of these bedding areas via one of these trails and attach your scouting camera to overlook a trail or convergence of trails.

Another daily need of a big buck is food. Locating your scouting camera overlooking a known feeding area is a terrific way of locating a big buck. This could be on an oak ridge where there are plenty of acorns or adjacent to an agricultural field. Better yet, set up your scouting camera to watch over a food plot, which is typically smaller than a full-fledged cornfield or bean field. Best of all, set up your camera over a concentrated food source such as a bait pile or feeder. This stacks the odds in your favor when it comes to finding a big buck.

Bucks have another tendency that serves to concentrate their whereabouts. Prior to and during the rut, bucks will make and visit both rubs and scrapes. By locating your scouting camera on the right rub or scrape, you are taking advantage of this tendency. Of course, like anything else, some rubs and scrapes will prove to be more productive than others. If you can find what is called a community rub, one of those rubs that are used year after year, you enhance your chances of getting a photo of the big buck you are looking for. Likewise, some scrapes are visited more often than others. Bucks will commonly use some of the same scrape spots year after year, as well. You can even make your own scrape (see chapter 7).

One of the best places to scout for big bucks is in their bedroom.

10/16/05 6:10 AM   Clare Hewitt   *Cuddeback*

Food sources are a good place to scout for big bucks.

10/25/06 8:47 PM   *Cuddeback*

Big bucks can also be located by setting up your scouting camera on the right trail. What is the right trail? Well, we hunters ask this question all the time. If the property you are scouting has one of those magic trails that seems to always be used, that is the right trail. Set your scouting camera to check it out for big buck travel. Big bucks love to travel through cover, so if your property has a corridor of cover that links a bedding area to food or one section of woods to another, trails within this cover are a good bet. Also, keep in mind that because your scouting camera can scout all night, those trails that you may never hunt during the day may be terrific spots to get a night photo of that big buck.

As crazy as it may sound, one of the best ways to get a photo of a big buck is to make a trail that a big buck simply can't refuse to use. You've probably

Trails between bedding areas and food sources are good places for your scouting camera.

Scrapes attract bucks, especially during the rut, which makes them terrific places for your scouting camera.

noticed if you hunt in the North that deer will frequently walk in your tracks after a heavy snow. Likewise, if you cut a convenient trail through heavy cover, deer will tend to use it. Better yet, cut that trail and rake it so deer can walk quietly and they will use it even more. Raked or cleared trails, whether manmade or natural, are excellent places for your scouting camera.

PROSPECTING FOR BUCKS

Okay, so you are not obsessed with finding that one big buck. But I'll bet you still want to know what bucks are on your property available for you to hunt. All of the tips delineated above in the big bucks section apply here. All bucks like the security of heavily covered bedding areas. All bucks need to eat. And all

8/15/06 2:34 AM   Dennis Larson   *Cuddeback*

During the summer, bucks travel in bachelor groups, making it easier to find out what's on your property.

bucks make and visit rubs and scrapes. Finally, all bucks take trails. If you truly are looking to find evidence of all the bucks on your property, though, bedding areas and trails are probably not the answer. You will want to concentrate your scouting camera efforts around food or scrapes.

Deer are social creatures. Their gathering spots tend to be associated with food. While the majority of the activity associated with food takes place under the cover of darkness, it is certainly not limited to the night hours. Bucks typically run in bachelor groups throughout the summer months. The deer in these bachelor groups will frequently visit food sources together. Because they travel together, this is a wonderful time to inventory the bucks out there. Too many scouting camera users don't put their cameras out until after the hunting season starts. They are missing out on a time of the year when bucks, because they are concentrated, are relatively easy to find. Don't make this mistake.

One of the most common comments from beginning scouting camera users who put a camera overlooking a scrape is, "I can't believe how many bucks visited this one scrape." A common misconception is that a single buck makes a scrape to attract does and that one buck is the only buck using that scrape. This is certainly not true. While every scrape is different, you'll find that several different bucks will likely visit any given scrape. In some cases, you may find that upward of fifteen or twenty different bucks will visit a scrape during the rut. The bottom line is that scrapes, like food sources, are hard to beat when it comes to prospecting for bucks.

ASSESSING A HUNTING SPOT
The average weekend warrior may only spend a handful of days hunting during any particular season. They are especially fortunate if they can spend ten

Scouting cameras allow you to monitor stand activity even when you are not there. Note the stand in the background.

Cuddeback Digital Camera 11/02/06   3:15 AM   Non Typical, Inc

or twelve days deer hunting each year. This means they don't really want to waste one of those precious days scouting out a new spot. This is where their scouting cameras come in. If I have a hunch about a new spot I will initially set up a scouting camera. Not only do I avoid wasting my hunting time, but I also eliminate the hassle of putting up a stand before I know the spot is worthy. Do not underestimate the value of letting your camera evaluate a spot. Think back to all of the times that you hunted a new spot only to find out that it wasn't all you hoped it might be. Then, add up all of the time you spent hunting a marginal spot plus the time you spent setting up your stand. Over the years you will have wasted an awful lot of hunting time. In other words, scouting cameras will make your hunting far more efficient and far more effective.

HUNTING MULTIPLE SPOTS AT ONCE

I am frequently torn between two or three spots on a given morning or evening. In the past, I'd spend so much time fretting about which spot to hunt that I was often late getting to my stand. No longer do I have to wonder if the decision I made was right. By letting my scouting cameras monitor spots while I am not there, I know I can easily determine if I made the right decision. Not only does this put my mind at ease but, more importantly, it gives me an education. Over time I have no doubt I have become a better hunter because I get more feedback on my decisions. Think about it. You hunt spot A and wonder about spot B and C. Spot A did not live up to its promise and you have your scouting cameras monitoring both spots B and C. It does not take much effort to see what you missed if you are using scouting cameras. In the past you had no way of knowing what happened while you were not there.

Most hunters neglect hunting in the middle of the day, which, during the rut, can be very good.

DETERMINING WHEN AND WHERE TO HUNT

Scouting cameras allow you to determine when a particular spot is being used. Virtually every scouting camera stamps the time and date on each image. Is your new spot a morning spot or an evening spot? Or is it good during both the morning and the evening? I've also used my scouting cameras to test the assertion that hunting during the middle of the day is worthwhile. Believe me, during the rut, given the right conditions, the middle of the day is frequently superior to the traditional morning or evening hunt. I had read that this was the case for many years but it took a particularly adamant friend and my scouting cameras to convince me. Today, thanks to scouting cameras, I am a firm believer in hunting during the middle of the day. I admit that I miss leaving the woods for a hot lunch and some storytelling, but thanks to my scouting cameras, I won't miss the thrilling midday action during the rut anymore.

Scouting cameras will also make your hunt more efficient by pinpointing precisely where deer are apt to travel. On more than one occasion, my scouting camera revealed that what I anticipated the deer might do was different than what they actually did. I have one stand set up in a rather unusual place simply because my camera showed the deer did not take the trail I expected them to take. Fortunately, when I checked the camera, virtually all of the deer were traveling an area well down the hill. This prompted me to quickly move my stand to a different tree that has proven to be the right tree. Once again, by letting my camera do the scouting, I ended up in the right place.

You'll also find that your scouting cameras will accurately tell you where deer enter and exit fields or food plots. Many times, what appears to be the

primary entry point to a field or food plot turns out otherwise. Again, you have two choices. Do the scouting yourself or let your cameras do the scouting for you.

HAVING FUN WITH YOUR SCOUTING CAMERA

Most hunters buy a scouting camera for some or all of the aforementioned reasons. During the process of using it as a hunting tool they invariably find that it's also just plain fun. Hunting is not only about bagging a big buck or putting meat in the freezer. It's also about all of the interesting occurrences and experiences. Likewise, you will find that using scouting cameras is not just about the big buck. You never know what you might see with your scouting camera. Whether you have your camera on a trail or food plot, overlooking a scrape, or in a bedding area, you will eventually get photos of deer doing some interesting things. These photos will provide you with great enjoyment.

After the season you'll probably want to find out which of the bucks survived. If you are fortunate enough to harvest a deer, put your camera overlooking the gut pile to see what creatures make it their meal. During the winter you may want to get a photo of deer in the snow. You may also want to find out when bucks drop their antlers. Come spring you may find yourself trying to get a photo of a strutting tom turkey or a newborn fawn. Or wood ducks in the wood duck house you made.

During the summer you might want to find out what is burrowing in your backyard. Or you might want your scouting camera to get images of the bear that visits your bird feeder. Scouting cameras also make good surveillance cameras. You might find yourself using your scouting camera to watch for tres-passers or to see who's fishing off your dock when you're not home. Of course, you want to get your scouting camera back in the woods as the bucks start growing their antlers. Then again, you may put your scouting camera overlooking your bear bait. The fun you can have with the scouting camera is virtually endless. In fact, if you are like most scouting camera users you'll eventually end up with more than one scouting camera. In the following chapters, you'll learn how to use your scouting camera to scout for deer. You'll find details on using your scouting camera to monitor trails, scrapes, rubs, food plots, feeders, and more.

CHAPTER 6
Tracking Trails

One of the first places a deer hunter will locate his new scouting camera is on his favorite trail. What better place, he reasons, to get a photo than on the trails that the deer commonly travel? More often than not, however, this deer hunter will be disappointed with the number of images of deer captured on that favorite trail. While a trail may look to be heavily traveled, one must realize that these trails have been used for years. If no deer walks this trail for the entire next year, the trail will still look well used. The key is to find the right trail. In other words, all trails are not created equal.

I speak from experience. In the early days of scouting cameras, I remember placing my cameras on what I perceived to be well-used trails, only to be alarmed at how few deer I actually captured on film. I remember being concerned that my favorite hunting area was suddenly devoid of deer. Fortunately, such was not the case. In time, my scouting cameras helped me learn how to select the right trails for scouting camera use and how to select the right trails for hunting. The two are not necessarily the same.

Today, I place my scouting cameras on trails in a few select situations. First, I put my scouting camera on a trail that leads to or from either a bedding area or a feeding area. Second, I like to put my scouting camera at the intersection of multiple well-used trails. Third, I definitely locate scouting cameras on trails adjacent to treestands from which I intend to hunt. Fourth, if I find a good-looking funnel area, I place my camera on a trail within the funnel to assess how often that funnel is used. (Funnel areas are any natural narrowings of the terrain that cause deer movement to be concentrated, or funneled.) Finally, I frequently make my own trail or manipulate existing trails in order to influence deer travel to my benefit. To determine the effectiveness of my efforts, I deploy a scouting camera on these new trails.

TRAILS LEADING TO OR FROM BEDDING OR FEEDING AREAS

Scouting camera use, like hunting, is a quest for efficiency. If you are like me, you love to spend time in the woods. With that said, time spent in the woods is a whole lot more fun when I am seeing deer than when I am not. I have learned that a trail adjacent to a bedding area or feeding area is much more likely to garner me numerous deer sightings or a large volume of scouting camera photos than trails not in the vicinity of food or bedding cover. Again, it is all about efficiency. Look at it from this perspective: where do you spend most of your time when you are at home? Probably more than one-third of your day is spent in or around your bedding area. Assuming you eat three meals a day, a pretty good percentage of your time is also spent in and around your feeding area. If you are like most Americans, you also probably spend a fair amount of time around your TV. Deer are no different. Other than the TV, that is. They spend considerable time eating, sleeping, or resting. That is why my scouting cameras are on trails near feeding and bedding areas. Really, the only thing better would be if deer had TVs.

Of course, not all feeding areas or bedding areas are equal, either. Crop fields and food plots are probably the most common feeding areas. Crop fields tend to be quite large, and you will have to spend considerable time walking the perimeter of the crop field, as well as the adjacent woods, to determine the best access trails. As a general rule, look for the best cover and areas that will both allow the deer to feed without human interruption and accommodate a quick escape. Depending on the crop, it will probably be relatively obvious where most of the deer feeding activity occurs. Simply look for the trail or trails that

Any farmer will tell you that a good place to find deer is in a crop field.

lead to that spot. You might wonder why you cannot just put your scouting camera at the food source. Well, many times I do. However, there are times that I do not want my scouting camera in plain view. Locating it back in the woods a little way will assure it is much less conspicuous. Likewise, once the deer get into the crop field, they tend to spread out. You will also notice that a primary access trail will sometimes turn into multiple finger trails as it gets closer to the field. By locating my camera on the primary trail, before these splits, I will end up with more photos.

Food plots are really just mini crop fields, and the same rules apply. I will frequently use my scouting cameras to get to know the deer movement in an area and to determine exactly where to plant my food plots. In other words, I reverse the process and locate my food plot where the deer have already proven they like to travel.

TRAIL INTERSECTIONS

If one trail is good, two or more trails are better. Given the choice, I will always locate my scouting cameras at the intersection of multiple trails in an effort to increase my odds of getting photos. Obviously, when you can use one camera to cover two trails, you're maximizing the efficiency of your scouting. But the intersection of two infrequently used trails is not as good as one well-used trail. The ultimate scenario is to find trail intersections adjacent to feeding and bedding areas. Again, the idea is to locate your scouting camera in areas that deer frequent. Once in that area, if you can take advantage of multiple trails at one time, your odds increase proportionately.

If one trail is good, an intersection of two trails is better.

1/25/07   7:24 AM   Deer Slayers   *Cuddeback*

TRAILS NEAR TREESTANDS

One of the biggest advantages of scouting cameras is the ability to show you what happens while you are not there. Most hunters have multiple stand locations on any given piece of hunting property. However, one can only hunt from a single stand at a time. Part of the fun of hunting is deciding which stand to hunt. Sometimes we make the right decision, sometimes we don't. When we don't, we second-guess ourselves. With scouting cameras, we are no longer left to wonder what might have happened if we had selected a different stand.

For me, part of the process of developing a stand site is determining where to place my scouting camera. Like you, I consider all of the variables when placing my stand: tree options, typical wind directions, shooting lanes, available cover, access to and from the stand, and where I will put my scouting camera. Each stand site should include a place for your scouting camera. By placing a scouting camera at each stand site, you can easily assess the deer activity there. Simply checking the camera enables you to determine if and when deer came by a particular stand.

It is important that you set your camera up to capture as many deer as possible as they happen by any given stand. Some stand sites are conducive to this, while some are not. That is why I always consider my scouting camera when setting up my stand.

TRAILS IN FUNNEL AREAS

Another way to achieve scouting efficiency, when it comes to trails, is to locate natural funnel areas. Swamps, ponds, fields, roads, and ridges are all examples of obstacles that can funnel deer movement. Like any creature, deer like to follow the path of least resistance. At the same time, deer prefer to stay in cover for security. So, for example, in the areas I hunt in the Midwest, I frequently find funnel areas created by ponds and swamps. One of my favorite hunting spots is a narrow piece of cover between a large woods and a large swamp. On either side of the cover there is some open grassland that the deer prefer not to cross, at least not during daylight. So to move from woods to swamp, the deer follow the natural bottleneck. The trail through this bottleneck is a prime spot for my scouting camera. My scouting camera has proven that it is also a prime spot for a stand.

Over the years I have also recognized that what is a funnel area to deer is not always obvious to me. What is perhaps my favorite stand, on a property I hunt in Iowa, is on a grassy hillside between a dense woods and a set-aside field where we have a food plot planted. I know it is a funnel area because I have watched many deer follow it. However, to this day, I admit I do not necessarily understand why the deer are being funneled. After watching enough deer follow the same route, and verifying this activity with my scouting cameras, I

Look for natural funnel areas. They make for good camera spots.

10/10/06 12:24 PM   Dan Jacobs   *Cuddeback*

finally put up a stand in one of the few available trees. The stand has proven, over the years, to be the best stand on the property.

MAKING TRAILS

I first heard of this idea from veteran deer hunter Mike Wheeler, who explained to me that he would literally create trails for the deer to follow. He explained that he would create a trail that would give him the very best chance, given his preferred stand location, to direct a big buck where he wanted it to go. Mike cuts the trail a yard wide and even rakes the leaves from it to entice deer to take it. I have had the opportunity to hunt with Mike on his property in Kansas and have seen these trails firsthand, and I can assure you that, when you make them and rake them, big bucks will take them. If you are certain you can travel scent-free, these raked trails do make for wonderful entrance and exit trails for hunters as well as deer. Unfortunately, I have a hard time getting myself to religiously rake trails. I know it works, but I get enough raking in my backyard.

While I have not gone to the same extent as Mike, there are certain situations where I cut my own trails in an effort to direct the deer. It really does work. More often than not, I find myself manipulating existing trails in an effort to concentrate the deer. For example, if I have an area where a trail splits, I will frequently block one of the trails with some heavy brush and clear the alternative trail, making it more appealing to the deer. Again, deer follow the path of least resistance. So when you find a trail on which you want to hunt or place your scouting camera, you might want to enhance the trail and deter deer from alternative routes.

By setting up
to take
quartering
shots, you
give your
camera more
time to
trigger.

9/08/06 12:04 PM

SETTING UP YOUR SCOUTING CAMERA ON TRAILS

Regardless of what type of trail on which you set your scouting camera, there
are some general rules that will assure you get the best photos possible. First
and foremost, never set your scouting camera perpendicular to a trail. Too many
scouting cameras lack the trigger speed that would assure that you actually get
a photo of the deer that walks by. So, to maximize the time that your scouting
camera has to trigger, aim your scouting camera so it is quartering the direction
of the trail. You will also find that an image of a deer that is quartering at or
away from you will give you a better view of the deer's antlers than an image
taken from the side. This way, the tines of the antlers are not covering each
other.

Also, make sure that your scouting camera is on the same plane as the trail.
If there are hills, it is important that you consider them when aiming your camera. Many scouting camera users make the mistake of mounting their camera
too low or too far away from the trail.

Finally, consider the direction your camera is aiming. If your camera will be
taking photos directly into a rising or setting sun, which is prime time for deer
movement, you may have some photos that are severely backlit. The flip side of
this is that you can sometimes get a beautiful and colorful sky in the background just before the sun comes up or just after it goes down.

Scouting cameras are frequently called trail cameras for a reason. Perhaps
the most obvious place to set up your scouting camera is on a trail, but remember that not all trails are equal. Make sure to put your scouting camera on the
area of the trail that maximizes your chances of photographing that big buck.

CHAPTER 7

Scouting Scrapes and Rubs

If you want to see what bucks you have on or passing through your property during the rut, setting up a scouting camera over an existing or mock scrape is the way to go. Another great place to set up your scouting camera is a rub.

SELECTING THE RIGHT SCRAPE

It is critical that the deer hunter select the proper scrape to set up a scouting camera; this will ensure images of the best-quality bucks. The activity at scrapes can start in early October and gets increasingly more active until the peak of the rut. At this time, the bucks will abandon scrape activity completely because they will be spending every waking moment looking for, following, and breeding every doe in estrus they can find. This activity will go on for several days until the bucks are unable to find any more hot does. Then they will return to scrapes until the second rut peak, which is approximately twenty-eight days after the peak of the first rut. Every doe that did not conceive in the first rut will come into estrus again. The bucks will again abandon scrape activity until the second rut peak is over.

It should be noted that almost 70 percent of scrape activity occurs during the darkness of night. The only scrapes that are freshened or revisited are what we call primary breeding scrapes. Scrapes that are renewed or freshened get visited on the average of every three to five days by the same buck. The most and best activity at a primary breeding scrape during the pre-rut will be just after a heavy rain or snow, because the bucks will want to freshen them up with their scent.

Recent research by biologists at QDMA (Quality Deer Management Association) has proven that several bucks will visit the same scrape. This includes $2^1/_2$-year-old subordinate bucks. A two-year project was conducted on two parcels of property, focusing on the scraping behaviors of a wild population of whitetail deer, using motion-activated video cameras that allowed them to

10/20/06 7:01 PM   Justin Fuchs

Scrapes are typically visited by multiple bucks, making them excellent spots for your scouting camera.

10/29/06 4:27 AM   Thad.Burkette

Bucks will frequently urinate over their tarsal glands to deposit scent into a scrape.

observe scraping behaviors twenty-four hours a day. It was believed from past research that only the dominant buck in the area created and revisited these primary breeding scrapes, but those studies were conducted on captive deer in a fenced area. This new research study proved that, in a wild population of whitetail deer, many bucks will visit and mark the ground by urinating across their tarsal glands and also working the overhanging branch.

All primary breeding scrapes will have an overhanging licking branch that hangs approximately thirty to seventy inches off the ground directly above the twenty-four-or-more-inch pawed-up area on the ground. Again note that these

Bucks require an overhead licking branch on which they deposit scent.

Sometimes bucks will go to great lengths to leave their scent on a licking branch.

are the only scrapes that a buck will refresh. If a buck is unable to rub the forehead gland on the top of his head, the pre-orbital gland in the corner of his eyes, and chew the overhanging branch leaving scent from his saliva, he will not revisit a scrape. A person can literally cancel a scrape completely by cutting off the overhanging branch.

Most primary breeding scrapes are found either just outside a big buck's bedroom or just outside heavy cover near areas with high doe concentrations, like a feeding area. I have had much better results setting up scouting cameras on the primary breeding scrapes just outside bedding areas, especially for the

You'll find that roughly 30 percent of all scrape visits will happen during daylight; 70 percent occur at night.

10/27/06   4:03 PM   Todd Reabe   CB1   *Cuddeback*

really mature, trophy-class bucks. It seems they will spend more time during daylight hours at these scrapes and visit them more frequently than others because they are so close to their thick-covered bedding area where they feel more secure. Because of their close proximity to the bedding area when they exit and enter the bedding area there is a much better chance it will still be legal shooting light. In general, by the time these big mature animals reach feeding areas it is well after dark. I truly believe from my studies that the primary scrapes close to feed areas receive less overall activity, especially during daylight hours. So the best scrape and location a deer hunter could select to put up a scouting camera is a primary breeding scrape outside a buck's bedding area.

HUMAN SCENT ELIMINATION
Before I begin to discuss how to set up a scouting camera at a mock scrape or an existing scrape, it is critical that I explain how important it is to eliminate as much human scent as possible. This includes entering and exiting the scrape site. The best way to describe this is that we must have the mindset of a fox or wolf trapper. These animals are so hypersensitive to human odors they would never go near a trap that left any sign of a human. When we set up our scouting cameras over an existing scrape or a mock scrape we are trying to trap the deer into a situation where we can get his picture and eventually hunt the buck. If we have this mindset up front, understanding how absolutely vital scent control is, we will do a much better job trying to eliminate it. Every time a human enters the deer woods he should be as scent-conscious as he would be if he were going to hunt that spot.

If at all possible, always shower and shampoo with scent-elimination products like Wildlife Research Center's Scent Killer products before entering the deer woods. I brush my teeth with baking soda and watch what I eat before I go into the woods. About a month before the deer season starts I start taking chlorophyll tablets because they really help with the different odors a body emits by neutralizing them in your system. Wearing a Scent-Lok Technologies total system including the head cover and gloves along with rubber boots greatly reduces the chance of getting busted by deer. Spray all of your equipment with Scent Killer spray and don't forget to spray the scouting camera housing before you leave. These products have proven themselves to hunters year in and year out. They have truly stood the test of time and helped us get close and go undetected by more trophy animals than ever before.

If all deer hunters paid more attention to all the obviously human smells they are carrying into the woods with them, and were just as careful about what they are leaving behind, they would be much more successful.

MOCK SCRAPE SETUP

It is possible to actually set up a mock scrape in an area, get bucks to come in to it, and turn it into an active primary breeding scrape. The first step is picking the proper location to set up the mock scrape. I like to set up several in different locations on a property because only about 25 percent of them will become active primary breeding scrapes. If you have thoroughly scouted and hunted the area previously and know where there was a very active primary breeding scrape, that will be a prime location to set up a mock scrape. The key to a mock scrape is that you want it to transform from mock to active as soon as possible.

When I create a mock scrape, the first thing I do is make sure I build the scrape under the same type of tree that the deer are using for natural scrapes in the area. For example, if the bucks are scraping predominately under a chokecherry tree, I'm going to locate a chokecherry tree in the area under which to create my mock scrape. I'm also going to make sure the overhanging licking branch is approximately the same height as the natural scrape's and always within the thirty- to seventy-inch range from the ground. I will also completely clip the overhanging branch from a natural scrape and secure it to the overhanging branch of my new mock scrape. All of the dynamics of the natural overhanging branch will now be incorporated in my mock scrape. I also will completely cut off the overhanging licking branch from all of the natural scrapes I no longer want to compete with and take them out of the area. By doing this, those scrapes will die out and no longer appeal to the bucks in the area.

After the natural overhanging branch has been firmly secured to the overhanging branch of the tree where I'm creating my mock scrape, I hang a Wildlife Research Center Ultimate Dripper loaded with their Active Scrape attractant,

A dripping
device can
entice deer to
use a mock
scrape.

just above the overhanging branch. I use a thick stick or garden rake to remove the debris from the ground directly under the Ultimate Dripper until I have freshened earth in a minimum of a two-foot circle. Paying particular attention to never kneel on the ground to avoid transferring scent through my pants where my knees touch the ground, I finish off the mock scrape by slowly pouring about two ounces of the Active Scrape attractant on the freshened earth directly beneath my Ultimate Dripper hanging above the overhanging branch.

SCOUTING CAMERA SETUP TIPS FOR SCRAPES

Several setup tactics will ensure that you are not disappointed with the pictures you get at scrapes.

- Always select a position on a tree that has the lens of your scouting camera facing north or south. This will ensure the light from the rising and setting sun won't wash out any pictures that are taken during that time of the day.
- Select a tree that is eight to ten inches in diameter to use to mount the scouting camera. This size of tree is very sturdy and will not easily sway in the wind. Later in the season, when all the foliage has fallen off the trees, a smaller tree can be used because the wind will have very little effect on the movement of the tree.
- Clear any weeds or other vegetation away from the front of the camera to avoid obstructing the view of the camera. This will help ensure you do not get pictures of weeds swaying in the breeze at the scrape.

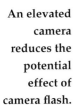

An elevated camera reduces the potential effect of camera flash.

7/30/06 9:52 PM *Cuddeback*

- It is important to be aware of the sensing capability of your scouting camera, and set it up within that range. If it is too far away or even too close, you will miss pictures. The ideal distance is somewhere between ten and fifteen feet. Be aware that during the cold weather of the winter some of the scouting cameras out there will sense out to as far as one hundred feet. This can be a problem because the cold temperatures combined with the darkness of the night will allow the camera in the unit to trigger outside of the range of the flash.
- When mounting the scouting camera at the scrape it is advisable to elevate the unit well above the eye level of the deer and have it angled down on the scrape, especially if you are using a scouting camera with a traditional flash. From our observations, a flash coming from above does not seem to worry the deer as much as one that is at their eye level or below. This may be because they all have experienced light from above during their lives from lightning storms and it does not seem to bother them unduly. This also applies to infrared scouting cameras. This can be critical if you are planning to hunt this scrape site in the very near future.
- Install new batteries when setting up the scouting camera. You will be very disappointed later to find out you didn't get many pictures because your not-so-new batteries went dead. Many people are switching to rechargeable batteries, claiming they last much longer than the traditional battery. Make sure you completely deplete them before recharging, however, as some batteries must be totally run down to fully recharge.

- Many times the images captured on the scouting camera will show a lot of buck activity at a scrape. When the buck activity at the scrape drops off dramatically, it is a good indication that the bucks are out chasing does and the peak of the rut is in full swing. At this time hunting the scrape will not be very productive.

Using a scouting camera on a scrape is similar to using one at a bait station, with one difference: there will not be nearly as much deer activity. In scrape scouting, the trigger speed of the scouting camera is much less critical, because deer will generally hang around long enough for the scouting camera to capture their image. However, battery life is critical in this situation not because of the number of images that will be taken, which could be very low, but because this is a setup where the person definitely does not want to miss any action. A scrape is one place I want to ensure I capture any deer with my scouting camera. I am not too concerned if I miss some deer when I have a scouting camera set up at a bait station or on a food plot because the deer will be back and my scouting camera will usually get another opportunity. But on a scrape, the window of opportunity is very short, with perhaps only a few days of heavy action. If those are the days the batteries are dead, I've essentially missed an entire hunting season, and perhaps a chance at the trophy buck that was ripping up the dirt on the scrape. Generally I have a handful of scrapes I'm scouting and I want to set up on the one that is being visited by the better bucks. Using a scouting camera will help me dial in the scrape over which I should be hunting. If my batteries are dead, I may end up hunting the wrong scrape.

Just a few years ago I captured an image of a great buck at a scrape on my scouting camera and immediately started hunting the scrape. I shot that buck just a day and a half later at that scrape. He scored $172^1/_8$. When you capture an image of a buck at a scrape, get in there and hunt it as soon as possible, while the window of opportunity is open.

When looking at battery life claims from scouting camera manufacturers, pay attention to how the manufacturer measures battery life. Some units will operate for a given number of images, say two hundred or fifteen hundred. If this takes a week or three months, the camera will get that number of images on a set of batteries. However, other cameras will operate for a set period of time, regardless of how many images are taken, say one week or three months. A scouting camera used at a scrape should have battery life longer than your planned checking period. So if you plan on checking the scouting camera weekly, make sure any unit you consider will operate for at least two weeks on a single set of batteries, assuming it will only take a couple of images at a time.

I always slip in during midday to build mock scrapes and to check the images on my scouting cameras. Remember, the images are going to tell you

A big rub can make for an impressive scouting camera photo.

11/03/06   1:59 AM   Clare Hewitt

two vital pieces of information: both the various bucks that are visiting the scrapes and, most importantly, when they are hitting the scrape. This information will help you decide where and when you want to set up your ambush.

SCOUTING RUBS
Of all the places to put scouting cameras, my favorite is at a rub. There is just something about watching a big buck working his antlers on the trunk of a small tree that I find compelling. And, compared with the other places we commonly place our scouting cameras—scrapes, trails, or food plots—rubs are visually distinctive and more attractive.

Rubs, like scrapes, are an integral part of the deer's mating behavior. Studies show that bucks make rubs from August through December, with September and October being the peak months. Rubs serve as signposts for bucks. By rubbing the bark from the trunk of a tree with his antlers, a buck exposes the lighter and brighter interior of the tree, which is visually noticeable to other deer. As a buck makes a rub, he will also deposit scent from the glands on his forehead. The resulting multi-sense signpost is an important part of communicating social status among the deer in the area.

You will typically find rubs along common travel routes. It has been my experience that putting a scouting camera along such rub lines, as they are called, will frequently result in photos of several different bucks. It will not necessarily, however, result in a photo of a deer working that rub. If you wish to get a photo of a buck working a rub you will need to find what is sometimes called a community rub. A community rub is a rub that gets worked year after year. Scientists feel that community rubs are more common in areas that have a balanced deer herd with numerous mature bucks. These community rubs typically occur on somewhat larger trees.

If you are one who hunts the same property year after year, you might already be aware of a community rub. I recommend that you place your scouting camera on that community rub starting sometime in August and keep it there throughout the rut, if it proves to attract deer. Odds are, if it is truly a community rub, you will find that several of the deer in your area, including some mature bucks, will visit this community rub. It is not unprecedented for a good community rub, in an area with a well-balanced deer herd, to be visited by a dozen or more different bucks in a short period of time. If you are fortunate, you will get an image of a big buck aggressively working your community rub.

You will also probably get images of a number of does scent-checking your community rub. Again, community rubs are signposts made of both vision and scent. Does, like bucks, are attracted to the scent left by bucks on a rub. You might also want to experiment with adding your own deer scent to a community rub. Keep in mind that a community rub has had scent deposited over a number of years and really does not need any more scent. However, adding scent can accelerate the use of a community rub.

An alternative to altering an existing community rub is to create a mock rub. With a tool, such as a hunting knife, rub a tree just as a buck would with his antlers. Then, apply deer scent. You'll find that this mock rub will sooner result in a photo of a buck than will placing your camera overlooking a random rub. Be sure to locate your mock rub where deer can see it.

Occasionally, I've seen photos of deer making a fresh rub. These photos are typically the result of a well-placed camera along a trail or field edge and a large dose of luck. The luck comes when the buck chooses to randomly rub a tree not previously rubbed. So, from a scouting camera standpoint, the value of a rub is to locate bucks. Assuming you can locate a community rub, a rub that will be visited throughout the rut by a variety of deer, you have a potentially successful scouting spot. Make sure you give it a chance to produce.

I like rubs because they are visually interesting. Truthfully, scrapes and licking branches are more reliable when it comes to attracting deer than even the best community rub. But, I'll take the aesthetic value of a rub photo every time. That is really why I put my scouting cameras on rubs.

A community rub that bucks visit year after year is a good place to locate your scouting camera.

Cuddeback Digital Camera 11/23/05 9:28 PM   Non Typical, Inc

If you are lucky, you'll get a rub photo like this.

11/02/06 2:12 AM

CHAPTER 8

Using Scouting Cameras with Food Plots and Feeders

O f all the ways to sway the odds in your favor when it comes to getting photos of deer with your scouting camera, using food is, by far, the best. As I recall from way back in high school biology, at the foundation of Maslow's Hierarchy of Needs are food, water, and shelter. While this refers to human needs, it also applies to deer. Fundamentally, food and water are the two basic necessities for any mammal to survive. Of these two, from a scouting camera standpoint, food is at the top of the list.

So if you want to maximize the number of scouting camera photos that you get, or if you want to increase the odds of getting a photo of a particular deer, use food as an incentive. This is not a new concept. If you want your teenage son to see your note, you post it on the refrigerator. If you enjoy seeing birds in your backyard, you put up a bird feeder. If you want to catch a furbearer, you use bait. Living things all tend to gravitate toward food.

FOOD PLOTS

In the last two decades, food plots have revolutionized deer hunting. Food plots are designed to do three things: first, food plots attract deer. By planting a food plot, you can effectively attract deer from your neighbor's property. Second, food plots provide the deer on your property with the necessary nutrients to give birth to healthier fawns and grow much larger antlers. And third, food plots concentrate the movements of deer, making them easier to pattern and easier to hunt. For all three of these reasons, food plots have become very popular with today's deer hunter.

Given that the scouting camera user wants to find a big buck, assess deer herd makeup, and pattern deer, food plots and scouting cameras were made for each other. The use of food plots is nothing new. Hunters have long realized that providing deer with readily available food made for a better deer hunt. Leaving a section of a cornfield up all year long was common practice among farmers who hunted. Hunters also realized that hunting adjacent to fields of

10/21/06   5:35 PM

Bait may be controversial, even illegal, but will definitely attract deer.

soybeans, alfalfa, and other crops was a good way to increase their chances of seeing deer. However, it has only been in the last two decades that commercially produced seeds designed specifically for planting food plots have become popular.

Food plot companies have gone to great lengths to create products that attract, grow, and concentrate deer much better than traditional crops. Food plot products today contain a variety of ingredients that deer find attractive all year long. Depending on the time of year, deer have different requirements. In the spring, coming out of winter, their bodies are preparing for giving birth or for growing antlers. In the fall, bucks especially look to add weight in anticipation of the rut and the coming winter. A good food plot product provides the nutrients deer need all year long.

Food plots themselves range from small, modest, hand-planted areas surrounding your tree stand to large ten- or twenty-acre tracts that require a tractor to plant. Food plot plantings range from seeds you get at the local co-op to scientifically formulated plantings made specifically for whitetail deer. Some food plot seeds are annuals, which means they require replanting each season, typically in late summer. Most commercially available food plot seeds are perennials, which means they come out on their own for three to five years before you need to replant. Regardless, any size or kind of food plot is better than no food plot at all, especially when you are trying to get a photo of a big buck.

Without question, more hunters have purchased food plot products with an interest in growing antlers than for any other reason. Protein is the critical component necessary for antler growth. If you look on a bag of food plot seeds, you will find reference to protein and antler growth. A good food plot product will

10/10/06 12:11 AM   Jeff Apprill   Cuddeback

Bucks are attracted to high-protein food plots, which help them grow big antlers.

Cuddeback Digital Camera 8/07/05 8:51 PM Brian Treb

Food plots serve to attract deer from neighboring properties, making them good places to photograph deer.

contain over 30 percent protein, which is necessary for optimal antler growth. The browse and crops that deer eat do not contain anywhere near this much protein. By supplementing what deer on your property eat on a daily basis with high-protein food plot plantings, you multiply the chances of being able to hunt a trophy buck.

Although this may sound like hype, all you need to do is look in the record books and you will see that far more record-class deer have been harvested in the past two decades than during any comparable time previously. In fact, the Whitetail Institute, the leading food plot company, says that according to their research, five times more record book bucks have been bagged in the last two decades. There is little question that the popularity of food plots, along with improved deer herd management, are responsible for these staggering statistics.

While attracting deer from your neighbor's property and providing your bucks with the protein necessary for larger antlers is important, the ability of a food plot to concentrate deer movement is probably its most important benefit to the scouting camera user. Because deer alter their movements by making food plots a focal point in their day-to-day routine, they become easier to pattern and to hunt, with both your scouting camera and your bow or gun.

Where to Locate Your Scouting Camera Relative to Your Food Plot
My first experience with hunting food plots was in Iowa. We hired a local farmer to plant our food plot seeds for us. We met with him in the spring while turkey hunting. We selected what to plant and where we wanted it planted and left him with the instructions. That fall, when we arrived to hunt deer, two of the three food plots were in sad shape. We ultimately determined that the problem was from a lack of packing down the seeds. The successful food plot was the one that the farmer happened to drive the tractor over several times, effectively packing the soil. We hunted the property as we always had, even adjacent to the successful food plot. Since the property was so far from home, we only deployed our scouting cameras once we arrived. It took the better part of the four-day hunt just to figure out where the deer entered and exited the food plot. There were far more deer in this area than ever before. That was the good news. The bad news was that they did not use the area at all as they had previously. It was four days of hunting education. We saw lots of bucks—some very large bucks—but none of them came past the stands we had always hunted. In fact, there was one spot in the middle of a grassy hillside that deer inexplicably used to enter and exit the food plot. None of us could recall ever seeing a deer come in or out of that field from that area before. The food plot changed everything. Today we still have a ladder stand on one of the few trees on that grassy hillside. It is probably the best stand on the property, year in and year out. The moral of the story is that it pays to use your scouting cameras to scout food plots before you hunt.

Hunting directly on or adjacent to a food plot is fine as long as the deer will come to the food plot during daylight hours. This is where your scouting cameras come in. Attach your scouting cameras to trees so that the cameras look down the boundaries of the food plot. This will allow you to determine not only where the deer enter the food plot, but also what time they enter it. Depending on hunting pressure, region, and time of year, some food plots may get minimal daytime activity. Do not use your hunting time to figure this out. If this is the case, you are better off hunting trails that lead to the food plot. If your scouting cameras show that deer do not use your food plot during shooting hours, follow the trails on which the deer come into the food plot back toward bedding areas. Here you can redeploy your scouting cameras. Now you will be able to pick the best trails based on the photos you get.

Odds are, deer, and especially bucks, will follow the heaviest cover to the food plot. Besides monitoring trails, be sure to monitor corridors of heavy cover. The heavier the cover, the closer to the food plot a wary deer will venture during daylight.

Natural funnels adjacent to your food plot are also worthy of scouting. Again, a food plot, especially a larger one, can become the hub of deer activity. If this is the case, natural funnels are ideal places to hunt. But before you put up your treestand, let your scouting camera do the work. And remember, things change as the season progresses. If, in August or September, that funnel area that looked so good before simply does not produce, be sure to check it out again during the rut.

If your food plot does get visited during daylight hours, you will probably find that deer enter from areas where they feel the safest. This means approaching from adjacent heavy cover where they can survey the situation prior to entering. My experience is that, all things being equal, deer will prefer to enter via a food plot's corners. Since most food plots are smaller squares or rectangles located in the ends or corners of larger fields, you will probably have one or two food plot corners that are also field corners. You will also probably have a food plot corner adjacent to a field edge. The food plot corner that is also a field corner will almost always be the best place for hunting. With that said, do not overlook food plot corners that are adjacent to field edges. I will always put a scouting camera in such a spot if the adjacent cover is worthy.

Use your cameras to find where deer enter food plots, then locate your stands on those trails, but back in the woods.

Cuddeback Digital Camera 8/07/05 6:59 AM Non Typical, Inc

I have also found that ridges paralleling the long sides of rectangular food plots get more deer traffic than they did before the food plot existed. In fact, during the rut, such a ridgeline will be hard to beat. During daylight hunting hours, deer will prefer to be in cover and will be more apt to follow existing trails. Most ridgelines have well-worn trails. Be sure to locate a scouting camera along such a ridgeline.

During a recent season of hunting on the property in Iowa, I located a scouting camera along one of these ridgelines. This particular ridgeline, the season before, had a remarkable amount of big buck movement. Our party harvested several of these bucks. My intention was to hunt the spot as soon as the rut kicked in. The first thing I did when I got to the property was to check the camera, which had been out for several weeks. I was astonished to find not a single respectable buck had been there. Perplexed, but forced to believe what the scouting camera did or, in this case, did not see, I hunted elsewhere. Never during that season did that spot produce a photo of a decent buck.

After the season I asked numerous experienced food plot hunters why they thought this had happened. One savvy hunter suggested that we had failed to change up our food plots. I asked him what he meant. He said it was his experience that if your property stays the same with respect to food plots from one year to the next that the deer grow tired of it and can be lured away to other nearby properties that have changed things up. In subsequent years, we have kept the deer interested by changing our food plot schemes. And, sure enough, that ridge has consistently produced nice deer. When I tell this story to others, most of them just shrug their shoulders. I do not think they believe me. It has,

Deer will frequently enter food plots in corners where they can see the entire plot.

Cuddeback Digital Camera   8/11/05   3:24 PM   Non Typical, Inc

however, been suggested to me that during its first year, a food plot is more appealing to the deer than in subsequent years. I do not know if this is true, but I can assure you that we do not want to find out. Therefore, we continue to add new food plots every year.

Food plots are, ultimately, probably the best place to get a photo of a phantom trophy buck. You will find that this buck enters the food plot because it is the best available food source. Or, he will enter the food plot because other deer are in the food plot, and they are there because the food plot is the best available food source. During the rut, this trophy buck is certainly out looking for a hot doe, and she is likely to be at the food plot at some point.

If you are only interested in using your food plot to locate a trophy animal, it is my opinion that you should deploy your scouting cameras in the food plot itself. Most people would attach their scouting camera to a tree and face it out into the food plot. The problem with doing this is that the majority of your photos will happen at night, which means your photos will have no background, just blackness. Also, by aiming your camera toward the woods, your flash will bounce back, illuminating the deer. By using a tripod and putting your cameras out in the food plot, aiming back toward the woods, you will get better images.

The best way to look at a food plot is from the perspective of deer. Their basic needs are food, water, and cover. First and foremost on that list is food, and the best food source is a food plot. This means the best place to look for deer is somewhere in the neighborhood of a food plot, and the best way to look for deer is with your scouting cameras.

FOLLOWING DEER AT FEEDERS

Using bait to attract deer for hunting purposes can be controversial. In some parts of the country, Texas for example, hunting over feeders is a common practice and an ethically accepted means of pursuit. Conversely, in my home state of Minnesota, it is illegal to hunt deer over bait. Next door, in Wisconsin, hunting over bait is legal, albeit controversial. The fact that hunting over bait is controversial should indicate, in my opinion, that it works.

Using bait to attract deer for scouting camera purposes is a different story. It is not, nor should it be, illegal. However, if you are going to use a form of bait for scouting, make certain that you check the regulations in your state before hunting that area if the bait or remnants of the bait remain.

Food or bait can take many forms. Here are some of the more popular and effective methods of attracting deer with food or bait.

Automatic Feeders

Perhaps the most sophisticated method of attracting deer with food or bait is with an automatic feeder. While such feeders vary in terms of features, the basic premise is that you load the feeder with food and set it to dispense that food at

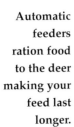

Automatic feeders ration food to the deer making your feed last longer.

11/30/05 8:58 PM   Curt Counts

Automatic feeders attract numerous species of wildlife, not just deer.

7/18/06   4:25 AM

preprogrammed intervals or times. Eventually, the deer, and many other critters, will learn when it is feeding time. Frequently, the noise made by these feeders in dispensing the food becomes a conditioned signal that it is time to eat.

The real beauty of automatic feeders is that they provide just enough food to keep the deer interested yet not so much food that the deer eat you broke. In other words, automatic feeders ration the food. Most of the deer on any given piece of property that utilizes an automatic feeder will readily come to that feeder to eat. Naturally, if there is a deer that does not feel comfortable coming

Cuddeback Digital Camera   8/02/05   9:29 PM   Non Typical, Inc

Feeders may attract deer, but they don't make for pretty photos.

to the feeder, it is usually a mature buck. If this is the case in your situation, make sure that you provide food during the night. Most of the time these mature bucks will feel more comfortable under the cover of darkness. You might also make sure that the feeder is adjacent to cover. Having a nearby escape route increases the likelihood that a mature buck will visit. Without question, using an automatic feeder will dramatically increase the number of deer that you will see with your scouting camera. The downside? I think there are three potential disadvantages of using an automatic feeder. First is the bait issue. Some people simply choose not to use bait, especially mechanized bait, while hunting or while scouting. Second is aesthetics. Virtually everyone prefers to get a photo of a deer in a natural setting as opposed to a photo of a deer with an automatic feeder in the background. Third is the potential for spreading disease among deer. There is theory among scientists that concentrating animals in a small area for feeding increases the likelihood of spreading disease. One will occasionally see a scouting camera image, for example, in which a deer or other animal is urinating on the food. Obviously, this cannot be healthy. When it comes to these issues, each one of us will have to make our own decisions.

Manual Feeders

In many cases, feeders are nothing more than containers that keep the food off the ground, keeping it dry and away from smaller animals. Using such a container also allows one to easily move the food source somewhere new, or remove it completely when it comes to hunting season. Such feeders are readily available commercially and can be easily made by hand with a piece of

Containing feed keeps it from spoiling.

plywood, some two-by-fours, and some nails. Just make sure that you do not have any exposed nails that may injure hungry deer.

You will find that with manual feeders you go through much more food than with automatic feeders, as there is no way to regulate how much food the deer and other animals eat. However, a manual feeder costs less than an automatic feeder, and that difference in cost can buy an awful lot of food.

As with automatic feeders, manual feeders will cause a large increase in the number of deer attracted to your property. You will also, however, incur the same disadvantages as with automatic feeders. You are baiting the deer, which concentrates feeding and, therefore, subjects the deer to potential health issues. And your scouting camera photos will still feature the deer as well as the feeder.

Bait Piles

Most scouting camera enthusiasts who employ the use of food or bait simply pour that food or bait on the ground in a selected area. The truth of the matter is that deer really do not care how the food is provided. Pouring the food on the ground does not seem to deter the deer—they like an easy meal. One advantage of simply pouring your food on the ground is that you do not have the unsightly feeder as part of your photos. Of course, an observant viewer will be able to see the bait on the ground, but most people find that far more acceptable than looking at a hunk of metal, plastic, or wood in the background.

Another advantage of using a simple bait pile is that you can easily move that bait pile to a new location, once it has been eaten. This way, you limit the deer's exposure to spoiled food. By simply moving your bait pile a short distance, you largely eliminate any such recurring exposure.

Cuddeback Digital Camera   7/29/06   8:40 PM   Chris Powell

One advantage of placing bait on the ground is that you can easily move your bait pile.

9/19/06   8:13 PM   Andy Lynch   *Cuddeback*

Deer love apples and apple trees make for wonderful camera spots.

NATURAL BAIT

Another way to increase the number of scouting camera photos you get is to set your camera up overlooking a natural source of concentrated food, such as an apple tree. We all know that deer love apples. Just ask an apple orchard owner or anybody who has an apple tree in their yard. I happen to live in suburbia, but on numerous occasions I have seen deer in my backyard. On every one of those occasions the deer were there to eat apples from my apple tree. I remember one September evening after just getting back from an Alaskan fishing trip. I was

Mineral stations are an excellent way to attract deer, allowing you to assess your deer herd.

5/27/07 4:53 AM

showing friends and family the photos of some big fish that I caught, but motion out the front window caught my attention. It was two very large bucks walking down the middle of the street, right past the streetlight. Everyone rushed to the windows to watch this unusual sight. The deer proceeded into my backyard, attracted by the apple tree. Pretty soon we were all walking around the neighbor's house and hiding behind their fence, mere feet from the unsuspecting deer. We could easily hear the deer chomping on the apples. I remember it all pretty well, not only because the bucks were so big, but also because nobody was interested in my fishing photos anymore.

So if there is an apple tree in your area, you will probably find that the deer come to eat the apples. There is no better place to set up your scouting camera, if your goal is to get lots of photos. You may also see some very large bucks, as the bait you are using is well liked and truly natural.

Of course, any other kind of fruit trees will attract deer, as well as acorns, garden vegetables, and a variety of other things. The bottom line here: if you find something provided naturally that the deer like to eat, you should put up your scouting camera and see what is coming to dinner.

LICKS AND ATTRACTANTS

Bait does not necessarily have to be food. There are hundreds of available licks and attractants that will bring deer in front of your scouting camera. Way back when I started deer hunting, salt licks were commonly used to attract deer. Today, there are commercially made licks and attractants in countless forms and flavors. There are liquids and powders and blocks. There is even a mineral supplement in the shape of a rock. Flavors can be sweet or salty, and include honey, persimmon, peanut butter, molasses, acorn, apple, sweet corn, and more. These products promise to provide protein, vitamins, carbohydrates, and fat. They contain calcium, sodium, magnesium, sulfur, potassium, phosphorus, iron, copper, and/or zinc. Besides attracting deer, these products claim to develop bone, grow antlers, help with milk production and even keep ticks off, among other things. So which lick or attractant should you choose? Your guess is as good as mine. Part of the fun of using these products in conjunction with your scouting camera is to try to figure out what scents or tastes attract the deer during the different seasons.

Scents

Deer scents are another category of attractants. As a deer hunter, you are, no doubt, aware of how many different scent alternatives are available. As with licks and attractants, the options are endless. Generally, attractant scents or lures will attract all deer. This is a good thing, even if you are looking specifically for bucks, because, especially during the rut, bucks are looking for does. Doe estrous scents are designed to attract bucks during the rut and, therefore, make good scouting camera attractants, especially when used in conjunction with scrapes. If you are looking for a trophy buck, consider using a dominant buck scent. Be aware, however, that the scent from a dominant buck may repel smaller bucks that do not want to get beat up. As with licks and attractants, it pays to experiment to find out what works best, and when.

There are several scent dispensers on the market that will make using scent to attract deer to your scouting camera more convenient. They can be as simple as highly absorbent cotton pads designed to disperse scent into the air as the wind blows, and as involved as drippers that claim to work only during daylight hours, thereby conditioning deer to check back during those same daylight hours. Of course, you can simply pour some scent on the ground, or onto a branch or some leaves. The dispensers are helpful in that they will prolong the effectiveness of the scent. This is particularly important when you consider that one of the key points of using a scouting camera is to stay out of the woods. If you are frequently going in and out of the woods to replace scent, you are defeating one of the purposes of your scouting camera.

The bottom line is that food and bait will attract deer to your scouting camera. The type of food or bait to use will depend on how much money you want to spend, and how much time and effort you want to expend. Simply put, if you want to get more photos, attracting deer with food or bait is the easiest way to do just that.

CHAPTER 9

Analyzing Your Scouting Camera Photos

So you have purchased some scouting cameras and learned how to use them. If you are like me, you probably put your first scouting camera out in the backyard and walked by it yourself to see if it worked. Then, you might have sent the family dog by to see if he would get his picture taken. Of course, the kids and their friends had to get into the act as well.

Your new scouting camera seems to work just fine, so you hook up to your computer or TV or maybe even your digital camera so that you can see the backyard images. Everyone looks a bit dorky, but you have proven that this scouting camera thing just might work. In fact, it might be kind of fun.

Next you plan your attack. Pondering where to put your camera is a lot like planning where to put your treestands or deciding which stand to hunt. This requires significant thought and is a big part of the fun. You consider all the variables and decide between all of the options you read about in previous chapters. Finally the decision has been made, and the cameras have been deployed.

You are not very patient, especially the first time your scouting cameras are out. You wait a whole day before you cannot stand it any longer. If you are lucky, you get a few photos and pull the memory cards to check them. If you are not, you have no photos and you kick yourself for being so impatient. After all, part of the beauty of using scouting cameras is that they allow you to scout without you having to be in the woods. You are not supposed to go back every day.

Eventually you fall into a pattern and learn how to best judge a reasonable waiting period between camera checks. But every situation is different and everyone's level of patience is different as well. The bottom line is that you are now getting photos, and probably lots of photos. They may be at your food plot, a trail overlooking a bait pile or a feeder, or even a scrape. Maybe you have photos of all of the above.

2/24/07 1:22 AM

Your "spies" will scout no matter what the weather.

11/23/06 10:08 AM

A key feature to a scouting camera is the time stamp on the photo, which shows you time of action.

Getting photos for the sake of getting photos is fine, but a scouting camera is a tool and every tool has a specific function. The specific function of your scouting camera is to provide you with scouting information: ideally, lots of information.

The intelligence you get from your scouting cameras can be divided into two categories. First is the information that you will use immediately to make short-term decisions. Second is the information that you will store to look for trends or tendencies over time.

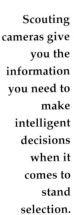

Scouting cameras give you the information you need to make intelligent decisions when it comes to stand selection.

A good analogy of the difference between the short-term information and long-term information is how a football team uses its scouting reports. If you watch much college or professional football, you have probably seen coaches and players on the sidelines looking at photographs that have been taken and faxed to them by the coaches upstairs. The coaches on the sidelines look at the formations that the defense used in the previous play or in a previous set of downs. Based on this instant feedback, the players on the offense will try to make use of what they have seen in these photos in the subsequent plays. This instant feedback is akin to you receiving some scouting camera photos from the last few days and making a hunting decision based on that information. That decision may be about which stand to hunt, which property to hunt, what time to hunt, or even whether to hunt at all. This information could be almost as timely as the information faxed to the sidelines. You may show up at your tree stand before first light in the morning and check your scouting camera on the spot. Based on what you see, you may climb into that stand or head off to a different stand.

Conversely, the football team typically spends the week prior to a game poring over game film of their opponents' previous games. The coaches are looking for trends and tendencies from which they can formulate a game plan. You can, and should, do the same thing with your scouting camera photos. This is your long-term analysis. By cataloging photos from various spots throughout the season, and from season to season, you will be able to look for trends and tendencies that allow you to formulate your own game plan. With this information, this intelligence, your decisions will be formulated based on cold, hard facts as opposed to gut instinct or memory.

11/04/06 8:40 AM

Outfitters rely on scouting cameras to put hunters in the right spot.

ANALYSIS BASED ON INSTANT FEEDBACK

Whether you have located your scouting cameras at a trail, scrape, rub, food plot, or feeder, the presumed purpose of that camera is to gather the intelligence with which you will make hunting decisions. If you are monitoring a stand site, sightings from several previous days are very important. Deer are creatures of habit, and while their movements change as the season goes along, there is a reasonably good chance that, if you get a photo of a shooter buck one day, he will be back in the days to come. At least you know that he is, or has been, in the area. If nothing else, you will know, with absolute confidence, that a deer worthy of hunting has been sighted in the vicinity. Just knowing this crucial bit of intelligence makes it much easier to spend time in the stand, even when it is cold or when you have other things to do. Often, this knowledge is the difference between a trophy on the wall and a big buck walking past an unoccupied treestand.

Likewise, a lack of deer sightings is also valuable intelligence. If your spies are not seeing deer in one particular stand or on one particular piece of property, you will know going in that if you sit in that stand, you are defying the odds. Obviously, this does not mean that you will not see deer. But it will sure make it more difficult to put your time in on that stand.

Outfitters, hunting clubs, hunters with multiple properties, or hunters with large properties and numerous stands will use scouting cameras to monitor many or all of their stand sites. If nothing else, they will be able to show prospective hunters what has been seen, where it has been seen, and when. The ability to use your scouting camera to monitor a spot also comes in handy at a brand new stand site. In the past, we would have to sit in a new stand to prove its worthiness. While sitting in a new stand for the first time may be interesting, it is also a good way to burn up a lot of valuable hunting time. I, for one, will opt for the spy every time.

ANALYSIS BASED ON LONG-TERM TRENDS AND TENDENCIES

Virtually every owner of a scouting camera uses it for making instant decisions. On the other hand, relatively few of us use our scouting cameras for determining long-term trends or tendencies. One big reason for this has been the cost and clumsiness of film. Digital scouting cameras are still quite new. I fully expect that long-term analysis will become more common, thanks to digital technology. The second reason that we scouting camera users tend not to use our information to its full extent is the need for manual analysis. One has to construct a system by which to conduct this analysis. Fortunately, this is changing. At least one company, Cuddeback, has introduced computer software specifically designed to organize scouting camera photos, which will allow you to conduct long-term analysis much more easily.

Called Trophy Room, this software allows one the ability to categorize each image according to multiple variables. In time, when you wish to look at all of the photos from a particular spot, for example, you will easily be able to do so, thanks to the software. Imagine being able to plot buck sightings at each of your stands over a period of several years. Might this information reveal that there are specific dates that particular stands are hot? Or will this information reveal that some stands are much better in the morning while other stands are much better in the evening? The possibilities are endless. The benefit of this long-term analysis is efficiency. You will be able to use the information provided by your scouting cameras to play the odds. Choosing where to hunt will be based on fact and statistical evidence as opposed to emotion and gut instinct.

The world of scouting cameras is changing. Thanks to digital technology, scouting cameras are now better tools than toys. These tools allow you to make better hunting decisions by providing you with information that you simply cannot get without them. This information or intelligence is pure in that it comes with no built-in bias. There is no human factor. You can use this information to make instant decisions by viewing your scouting camera images in the field. Plus, by using the software that has only recently become available, you will be able to analyze the information provided by your scouting cameras and determine long-term tendencies and trends. This, perhaps more than anything, will fuel the use of scouting cameras in the years to come.

CHAPTER 10

Scouting Cameras All Year Long

Too many scouting camera users pack their cameras away after the hunting season is over, not to see the light of day until the beginning of the following season. This is too bad, as they are missing out on a lot of useful information and great entertainment. Just for fun, I decided to count the number of submitted images in the Cuddeback scouting camera photo contest for each month. As one would expect, the months of October, November, and December had far more photos than any other time of year. August, September, and January are also prolific months, but there were still only one-third to one-half as many images submitted as during the peak months. I also noticed that most of the January images were actually taken during October, November, or December. The months from February through July saw even fewer submitted images, and a pretty healthy portion of those images were actually taken the previous fall. All of which proves that, after hunting season, most scouting cameras are relegated to the garage or basement.

During the film era of scouting cameras, I could see why hunters would not want to burn expensive film when it was not going to have a direct impact on the hunt. But, with today's digital technology, which eliminates the film and processing costs associated with using the scouting camera, there is no reason not to leave your scouting cameras out all year long. You just never know what you might be missing.

POST-SEASON SCOUTING

I know for fact that many hard-core scouting camera users keep their scouting cameras in the woods immediately after the hunting seasons are over. Big bucks are still carrying their antlers, and these hunters want to know which deer made it through the hunting season. In essence, scouting for the next season starts the day the current season ends. In many cases, these hunters already have a pretty good idea of where these big deer are and what they are doing. There is no better time, then, to verify exactly which big bucks will be available

An often-overlooked use of scouting cameras is to find which bucks survived the hunting season, to be hunted again next season.

12/27/06 10:19 PM   Clare Hewitt

to hunt the following season. There is no reason to wait until late summer, when the antlers have finally grown to the point that you can identify a big deer, to start this process.

Over the years, my involvement in several scouting camera photo contests has allowed me to read countless letters accompanying the photos. The passion and excitement of a trophy hunter who has captured an image of a post-season trophy deer that he will be able to hunt the next season is unmatched. Think about it: it is January and you already know there will be a monster waiting for you where you hunt next fall. Immediately following the hunting season, the best place to get a photo of a big buck is at a food source. These big boys will probably be relatively nocturnal, especially if they exist in an area with any amount of hunting pressure. Days are short this time of year anyway, so I suggest catching up with the big guy where he can get an easy meal.

WINTER SCOUTING

As the snow flies and the temperatures plummet, those deer that made it through the hunting season face a new challenge: surviving the winter. Because survival is largely dependent on food and because deer tend to herd during the winter months, the scouting camera enthusiast has the opportunity to put his cameras out where deer are naturally concentrated. Of course, it is feast or famine. If the deer congregate on your property, or if you know where the deer might come together, you have the chance to get a lot of great images. You also have an increased chance of getting a photo of your trophy deer. Some hunters

Deer in the North typically yard up as snow and cold make food hard to find. This makes for a scouting camera opportunity.

Snow makes it easy to get a good look at a big buck.

choose to feed the deer during the winter, thereby enhancing their photo opportunities even more.

In the North, where I live, the bucks typically keep their antlers until Valentine's Day. Sure, there are deer that lose their racks as early as late December, likely due to stress, but this is the exception. Likewise, it is not unprecedented to have deer maintain their antlers into late March. So you will probably have a couple of months to get in some wintertime scouting with your cameras.

One big advantage of scouting during the winter months, at least in the North, when and where there is snow, is contrast. It is far easier to see and assess deer body size and antler size when photographed against a background

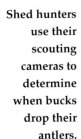

Shed hunters use their scouting cameras to determine when bucks drop their antlers.

1/24/07 4:57 PM   Rick Arnold

of snow. The same photo taken against a background of brush and trees is far more difficult to assess. Snow also makes for prettier photos, especially if taken during the day.

Another terrific reason to keep your scouting cameras in use during winter months is to monitor antler loss. If you are lucky enough to have a big buck in your scouting camera sights, surely you want to be the first to know when that big buck has lost one or both of his antlers. There is no better way than to scout that big buck with your scouting camera. Again, I have received numerous letters from lucky hunters who have used their scouting camera to determine when a big buck has shed an antler or two. With this information the hunter knows exactly when to begin his shed hunt, and the hunter can beat other potential shed hunters to the punch.

SPRING SCOUTING

To me, and to many other scouting camera enthusiasts, capturing images of a single deer year-round is a big part of the fun. In the spring, as bucks start to grow their antlers, I look to get the first images of a given deer and I hope to document his antler growth through an entire season. It is also during spring scouting that I like to see does with their fawns. If does have single fawns, it tells me that they have had a stressful winter. Twin fawns indicate a healthy and relatively stress-free deer herd.

There is also something uniquely magnificent about photos taken in the spring. The new green growth is so vibrant and alive that photos taken during this time of the year exude this vibrancy. Some of my favorite scouting camera

Cuddeback Digital Camera   7/04/06 12:02 AM   Non Typical, Inc

When does have twin fawns, it indicates the herd is healthy.

photos do not necessarily have trophy bucks as the subject. Rather, they are of does and fawns on a beautiful, sunlit, spring day.

SUMMER SCOUTING

Once summer arrives, antlers become the focus of the scouting camera hunter. The does, because they are tending to their newborn fawns, have chased the yearling bucks away. The small bucks, abandoned, tend to gather together in what are called bachelor groups. Mature bucks also gather together during the summer in bachelor groups. Typically, the yearling groups and the mature groups do not mingle. The fact that bucks are traveling together spells opportunity for the scouting camera user. Again, it is feast or famine. If these groups travel on your property, you stand a chance of getting a lot of great photos of bucks with their growing antlers. If not, you may only get an occasional photo of that ornery big buck that does not want to hang out with the boys.

It is not difficult to tell, even early on, whether a set of antlers is going to be impressive or not. Antlers grow quickly in the long June photoperiod and continue to grow throughout the summer, which is why it is valuable to get photos during the summer. You will absolutely be able to tell, relatively early on, if a buck is going to be a bruiser.

By late August, as days have gotten shorter and nights have gotten cooler, antler growth quickly subsides. Hard antler begins to protrude from the velvet. By now, you really should have your scouting cameras deployed. Bucks are still in their bachelor groups, but not for long. If you put your scouting camera overlooking a licking branch, you very well might get an image of a buck working that licking branch, perhaps even in velvet. Bucks do visit the licking braches

Young bucks are chased away by does in the early summer and join together in bachelor groups.

7/17/07 2:27 AM

Even in the summer, it is not difficult to recognize what will be a magnificent buck.

6/15/07 6:27 AM   Chad Oliver

overhanging scrapes as early as September, presumably due to the increased testosterone in their systems.

In early September, if you are lucky, you may get a photo of one of the most dramatic visual events in the life of a deer. It is typically during the first week of September, in the North anyway, that a buck will lose his velvet. This event seldom takes more than a couple of hours, but if you capture a photo during this time it can be impressive. The bloody velvet hangs from the antlers,

By late summer a buck's headgear is almost fully developed.

It does not take long for bucks to shed their velvet, so getting a photo like this is special.

revealing a blood-soaked rack. The buck will rub his newly exposed antlers to get rid of the velvet.

As I mentioned before, with the advent of the digital scouting camera, there is no reason not to leave your scouting cameras in the woods all year long. Not only will you probably be able to find the big buck you can hunt during the coming season, but you will also likely get some very entertaining photos. Keep those cameras out in the woods all year long!

PART THREE

CHAPTER 11

Informal Herd Surveys

I purchased my first scouting camera about fifteen years ago—a 35 mm film unit. There was a large parcel of private property in the Berkshire Mountains of Massachusetts abutting a state forest that I had been hunting for several years. The state forest always produced some great bucks, and I had already taken a couple of nice 140 class bucks from the parcel I called the "Honey Hole." I couldn't wait to get into the area and set up my scouting camera to get some pictures of the bucks that I knew were crossing back and forth across the boundaries of the two large parcels of property. I got some good pictures of bucks and many does from the different locations where I had set up my unit. I would drive my wife crazy talking about getting back out there to retrieve my film so I could get it developed. I just couldn't wait to see the pictures, and never realized at that time there was so much more that could be done with these great new scouting tools besides just taking pictures of the deer.

A deer hunter doesn't need a degree in wildlife science to make key discoveries about the deer that are roaming around on a piece of property. Any hunter can do this just by using a little brainpower and very minimal exertion of effort. The education a deer hunter can attain from using a scouting camera can improve the deer herd on his property and also the overall success of the hunter. The best part is that it will bring a lot of enjoyment and satisfaction.

We learned that the scouting camera will help any deer hunter develop strategies, and making sense of all the images captured with the scouting camera will play a key function in molding hunting tactics, making management decisions, and finally achieving better success in the field. The pieces of the jigsaw puzzle a scouting camera offers will provide the most accurate look into the very secretive life of the whitetail deer on a parcel of property.

Any deer hunter can use a scouting camera to conduct an informal deer survey of a property. You may remember the mark-recapture method of estimating population from your ecology class, for example. To apply this method, use a scouting camera to capture and identify the number of deer in a given period of time. Then, after allowing some time to pass, you re-deploy your camera and count how many deer you capture the second time around. You also identify how many deer were captured both times.

Now, using the Lincoln-Peterson equation, you can get your population estimate:

$$\text{Population} = \frac{(\text{Total captured first visit}) \times (\text{Total captured second visit})}{\text{Number of deer captured on both visits}}$$

For example, if you got photos of 15 deer on your first effort and 10 deer on your second effort, and 5 are "recaptures," you would multiply 10×15, and then divide by 5 for a population of 30.

Of course, this requires that you can distinguish among deer. While this is relatively easy with antlered bucks, it is more difficult with does.

HOW TO CONDUCT AN INFORMAL HERD SURVEY

An individual can get a basic idea of the deer on his property by using one or two scouting cameras to determine population, sex ratio, and fawn crop in both the northern and southern sections of the country. This informal survey will in no way give individuals the same degree of accuracy as conducting a formal deer survey (we will explore that information in the next chapter), but it will give a basic idea of how to estimate population characteristics on a piece of property. Although population is defined as all the individuals of one species present in a specific unit of area at a given time, the truth is very few landowners control a population that can be surveyed on a hundred acres or even a few hundred acres. When wildlife biologists or managers conduct a deer survey they are basically taking a snapshot of the property at that time. An individual can use one scouting camera on a smaller tract in the same location every year to compare relative data.

The total acreage in a parcel of property doesn't matter, because the deer are continuously moving back and forth across the boundary lines. This is very important to keep in mind while conducting surveys, analyzing the data, and making the management decisions for harvest quotas.

It is essential to keep in mind when employing any deer survey technique that the results from any one survey period are not as important as the trends that can be isolated over time. These trends will become obvious by using uncomplicated bar graphs to show the deer herd demographics.

Deer surveys should always be conducted at the same locations utilizing the same techniques from year to year and the comparative data will show what direction the deer herd and management program is headed.

The number of scouting cameras needed for this project will depend on how many different habitat types are on the parcel of property to be surveyed. If

Scouting cameras can be used to determine the makeup of your deer herd. Perhaps there is a shortage of does in this area.

10/22/06 5:32 PM

we assume there are two or three major habitat types it will be safe to use one or two units. On large tracts of land the best results will be obtained with at least one scouting camera for every hundred acres. It is important to note that on small parcels of property, where a hundred or fewer acres of land are being surveyed, the results will be buck-dominant. In fact, the smaller the parcel the more buck-dominant the results will be unless the area is under a high fence and the cameras are moved to different locations during the survey period. Any survey that is done with one scouting camera on any parcel over two hundred acres will be totally unreliable.

On informal surveys for small properties, use trail sets instead of bait stations for free-ranging deer, unless it is a high fenced small parcel of property under two hundred acres. Always make sure to pre-bait the camera stations prior to initiating the deer survey to insure the deer have found the food in those high fenced situations.

It is critical to place the scouting camera where the deer are at the time of the survey. It is best to grid the property into hundred-acre plots and set up the scouting camera in the best locations within that grid.

A few tips that apply to all scouting camera placements remain equally as important when conducting surveys: when selecting a camera site look for areas that have the heaviest deer activity. Look for spots where the deer tend to hang out, like trails, rubs, scrapes, edges of food plots, mineral licks, sources of water, edges of bedding areas, and agricultural fields. It is very important to clear the vegetation in a ten-foot radius to minimize the camera snapping an image of a branch or tall weed blowing in the wind. Always position the unit on a solid tree in a position facing north or south to avoid the glare of the sun and

9/18/06 8:39 PM

Locate your cameras in high-traffic areas such as at mineral stations.

backlighting in any of the images. Also set the bottom of the scouting camera twenty-four to thirty inches from the ground to avoid non-targeted animals. It is wise to keep notes on precisely how the unit is set and adjusting the setup until you have it perfect. This will help all the setups in the future.

When setting up trail sets, scouting cameras should be placed on the trails leading into a food plot or feed area. The number of images captured daily will be greatly reduced on the trail sets versus baits. The total survey duration should be between ten and fourteen days to provide adequate sex ratio and fawn crop results. It is also important to set the delay setting on the camera to ten minutes to ensure several pictures of the same deer are not taken. The time of year the survey is taken is also important. In the fall it is best to evaluate the bucks on the property because the antlers can be seen in the images. This information can give a basic idea of the age structure of the bucks and can also be used to make management decisions on what animals should be harvested from the herd. For the most accurate results about population, fawn crop, and sex ratio, late winter or early spring is the best time to survey a property.

35 MM OR DIGITAL: WHICH IS BEST?

Researcher Jason Snavely conducted a deer survey experiment utilizing 35 mm and digital infrared-triggered scouting cameras to reveal the advantages and disadvantages of both. His goal was to determine which camera system would produce the most images and finally the most accurate deer survey of a herd. He wanted to verify if more mature bucks would be caught with the digital units because the changing of film is not required and human disturbance at camera locations is greatly reduced. Also, he selected a parcel of property with

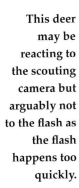

This deer may be reacting to the scouting camera but arguably not to the flash as the flash happens too quickly.

an extremely high deer density so he would get as many images as possible during the survey period.

He used a total of twelve scouting cameras for this research project, which included six 35 mm and six digital units with a camera density of one unit per fifty-seven acres. After the fourteen-day survey he obtained a total of 3,448 images of 4,808 deer. The breakdown results were 1,103 images of bucks, 1,967 does, 1,090 fawns, and 648 unidentifiable deer, which he excluded from the results.

Of the 3,448 total images, 1,106 images or 32 percent were captured on film scouting cameras while 2,342 or 68 percent were captured on digital units. These results showed the digital units captured over twice as many images as the film units. Of the 1,103 images of bucks, 209 or 19 percent were captured with the film units and 894 or 81 percent were captured with the digital units. This is more than four times as many digital images of bucks captured from the digital units during the total survey period.

The number of false events or non-target animal images differed slightly and should be investigated further. The results from the film cameras for false events were 134 images or 12 percent of the film images and 163 images or 7 percent for the digital units.

Snavely thought it would be useful to review all the images of the deer for camera reactions or flash fright. Any deer caught bolting away from the camera in an image cannot possibly be reacting to the flash of the camera, which is synchronized to the opening of the shutter on the camera. The photograph would be taken by the time a deer could even start to react to the flash of the camera. The deer seen reacting in images could be responding to the mechanical noises of the camera itself. The auto focus, film advance, and shutter mechanism are a few of the noises produced within the camera before the picture is taken. After reviewing the images with the 4,808 deer captured in the survey, Snavely found only 7 that displayed any negative reaction to the camera; one, a 4-point yearling buck, was captured a total of nineteen times during the duration of the survey before and after his negative experience.

Snavely's research findings suggest that mature bucks are more likely to avoid areas with film camera units because of the smell of the film. Although he was unable to prove or disprove that theory with this data, he suspected that more buck images were captured from the digital units for the following reasons:

- Digital scouting cameras operate 24/7, provided they have fresh batteries, because they never run out of film.
- Digital units require less maintenance since there is no film to check or replace, which results in a reduction of human disturbance where the units are placed.
- Bucks, especially those that are mature, may be more sensitive to the shutter and film-winding noises associated with the 35 mm film camera units.

Although the total number of digital images of bucks and mature does far surpassed the number of images captured from the film units, Snavely captured more fawn images from the film units. It was not a significant difference in the total number of images, but it may suggest from these results that film units are visited somewhat less often by mature deer for one reason or another. Fawns, seemingly much less cautious, did not hesitate to visit the film camera locations. This theory needs much more investigation.

The advantages and disadvantages of digital and 35 mm film infrared scouting cameras compiled during this survey follow.

Digital Advantages:
- No downtime because they never run out of film
- Fewer maintenance hours are required to keep the unit in operation
- Fewer checkups, which means less human disturbance at the unit location
- Images are easy to share via email
- Sharper images
- Larger memory cards can hold up to sixteen hundred images
- Identifying a buck by his antler configuration is much simpler with the magnification tools available on any computer
- No time spent driving back and forth to get the pictures developed
- Actual in-the-field image recovery is possible with a portable television, camcorder, or camera phone

Digital Disadvantages:
- Upfront costs are higher for purchasing the scouting camera, memory cards, and PC card reader
- Images have to be printed to make a side-by-side comparison

35 mm Film Camera Advantages:
- Side-by-side image comparison is easy

35 mm Film Camera Disadvantages:
- Missed image opportunities after 24 or 36 exposures of film
- Require many more hours to maintain
- More time in the deer woods causes more disturbance
- Lower-quality images
- Images must be scanned or put on a CD at a photo lab to share attached to email
- Require more time and money running back and forth to get the images developed and purchase new film

The overall results from the comparison proved that digital infrared triggered units are much more cost effective, less intrusive, and provide more accurate results than film units. Digital infrared triggered scouting cameras save time and overall cost in the long run and they stand sentry for much longer periods of time in the deer woods.

Scouting cameras allow you to assess what is on your property, which allows you to make good herd management decisions.

I cannot remember all the times over the years that I was in a deer camp or with a bunch of hunters and the conversation tended toward the subject of how to figure out the number of deer in the area, the buck-to-doe ratio, age structure, and the fawn crop. The conversation most always ended up in a disagreement because no one could agree on the number. With just a scouting camera and a little time, any deer hunter can come up with a basic idea of what is roaming around the property he hunts. It is a guarantee that you will get pictures of bucks that no one ever knew existed on the parcel of property. In the end you may be able to settle all the years of disagreements with the other hunters about deer numbers and where the big bucks are on a property.

A scouting camera will allow a hunter to enter into the hunting season much better prepared for the actual hunt, because he will know what the deer are doing. He will know where they are bedding, where they are feeding, and which trails they use to travel throughout their range. However, a scouting camera will not guarantee success for the hunting season. Mature bucks are sensory machines, with excellent senses of smell and hearing, as well as an uncanny ability to detect a threat. The sheer enjoyment of using scouting cameras goes beyond the hunting. It also provides a fascinating look at what is going on in the woods.

CHAPTER 12

Formal Herd Surveys

Any landowner or club can duplicate the more sophisticated deer herd survey techniques developed and used by wildlife biologists today. All it takes is enough scouting cameras and a little effort, and you'll get to know the dynamics of the deer herd on your property.

Why is it important for wildlife biologists and managers, clubs, or just property owners to know how many deer are roaming the woods? If they have this information they are better able to make management decisions that will improve the health of the deer herd or the production of quality trophy animals. The whitetail deer populations in North America have greatly increased over the last twenty-five years. In many places the numbers have grown to the point that they are problems as well as trophies. Furthermore, as the management strategies for deer increase, there will be an amplified call for more reliable and cost-effective techniques that will better approximate deer population characteristics.

Many techniques have been developed over the years by biologists and researchers to estimate the deer population, density, age structure, and buck-to-doe ratios of an area. A partial list includes aerial surveys, harvest-based estimates, spotlight counts, and most recently the infrared-triggered scouting camera. There are limitations that exist for every one of the methods and no single method is 100 percent accurate for conducting a deer survey. However, the infrared-triggered scouting camera method (IRT Method) has revealed enormous potential as an accurate survey approach.

INFRARED RESEARCH

Wildlife Biologists William McKinley and Jason Snavely described to me a simple, yet no-nonsense procedure to estimate the number of deer on a parcel of property as well as important herd characteristics including fawn crop, buck-to-doe ratio, and age structure.

The deer population in North America has flourished to the point of deer becoming a nuisance in suburbia.

Cuddeback Digital Camera   1/12/06   4:50 PM   Scott Kraus

Snavely doesn't like to use the word census because he feels a deer census is a complete count of every deer on a piece of property, and as anyone would guess, this is not possible. A biologist will estimate the deer densities in distinct areas then expand those numbers to obtain population estimates of much larger areas with similar habitat types.

This method will provide a wealth of useful information on a deer herd, particularly if it is used in combination with harvest data, observation data, and habitat evaluations. Through their research studies, these biologists have proven that a camera density of one per 100 acres provides adequate reliability to make very sound management decisions. McKinley's research studies have shown that a camera density of one per 160 acres decreases the level of accuracy by roughly half of the value and a camera density of one per 200 acres or higher is unreliable for parcels of 3,000 acres or more. On a small management area of less than 1,000 acres it is advantageous to have a camera density of one per 100 acres or less. For optimal survey results, there should be a camera density of one per 50 acres.

The researchers have concluded that a pre- and post-hunting season survey of the herd is most desirable. Pre-season surveys should be conducted just prior to the hunting season in September. Post-season surveys can be done immediately after the hunting season has concluded or before the bucks cast their antlers. When it is properly conducted, the post-season survey provides extremely acceptable results in all habitat types. However, when the survey is conducted pre-season, it is generally buck-dominant, underestimating the doe count and inadequately estimating the fawn count. This information can be used to determine which bucks should be harvested during the hunting season.

Pre-season
surveys
should be
conducted
just prior to
hunting
season.

The pre-season survey normally provides a more adequate representation of the bucks on the property but should not be used for population estimates unless there are several years of information available for pre- and post-season numbers. With this information, the degree of error from the pre-season survey can be determined and adjustment factors can be added to attain pre-season population estimates.

We must recognize that all population estimation methods involve a certain amount of assumptions. As an example, if the bait used to draw deer to the location is not attractive because a preferred natural food source is available, not enough images will be captured of the deer. Dr. Stephen Demarais, professor at Mississippi State University, believes the percentage of the population surveyed will vary between areas surveyed. He points out the assumption that the bait used is uniformly attractive to all the deer in the area. Is a doe just as likely to come to the bait as a buck, and vice versa? Also, as the mast crops and forage vary from year to year, so can the attractiveness of the bait used to attract the deer to a camera location.

McKinley and Snavely started their research with an aerial or topographical map of a property. For optimal survey results, they laid out the map to grid the property into approximately hundred-acre blocks. (It is not critical to be exact, just a good approximation of hundred-acre grid blocks will work.) McKinley explained that it is important to place the scouting camera units in locations that deer are continually using. It makes no sense to place a scouting camera in the middle of some thicket of cover just because it is the center of a hundred-acre grid. Old logging roads, water sources, agricultural fields, corners and edges of food plots, mineral licks, scrapes, rubs, along with any heavily used trail are

4/13/02   8:47 PM

Bait, unlike scrapes, is uniformly attractive to all deer.

good locations to set up a unit. There may be times that you use two scouting cameras only three hundred or four hundred yards apart in different hundred-acre grid blocks, because the deer are frequenting the area.

You may also utilize a GPS unit's waypoint for each scouting camera location. This will make it simple to create maps and to find the exact spot each year when conducting subsequent surveys.

The scouting camera locations should be cleared of debris and vegetation in a ten-foot radius. This will significantly reduce the possibly of false images by capturing a photo of a weed or branch blowing in the breeze. Utilizing a weed whacker will clear an area of all the vegetation in just a few minutes.

Always test the camera's field of view to ensure the background is adequate to identify deer up to fifty feet or more away from the camera's lens. Often multiple deer will appear in an image, not just the individual deer that triggered the camera. The bait sites should also be selected with that in mind. If at all possible, select locations that have constant lighting conditions. Avoid spots that are always partially shaded or only partially open to the sunlight.

Once you have chosen and prepared the location, attach the scouting camera unit to a solid tree, T-post, or other suitable stationary object, facing north or south to stay away from backlighting and any sun glare in the images. It may be advisable to carry a good compass along to ensure a north or south direction with each setup. Also, positioning the bottom of the unit approximately twenty-four to thirty inches from the ground will reduce images of any undesirable animals such as raccoons. It takes a little practice to perfect the best position. Adjust the unit setup and always take notes for future reference.

McKinley suggests numbering each scouting camera location with a glow-in-the-dark, stick-on number similar to the ones used on mailboxes and houses. Place the number on a small piece of plywood or metal and securely mount it to something in the background so it will show in every image captured. Also, instead of programming your name into the cameras, use the number placed at each location. This will be enormous help for record-keeping and identifying each scouting camera location on a map.

Snavely always carries a small backpack with him that is strictly for the scouting camera equipment so that nothing is forgotten back at the truck. This is a list of the recommended items to include in the daypack:

Extra rolls of film or flash memory cards
Camera batteries
Monitor batteries
Bungee cords, string, and straps for larger trees and any awkward setups
Scouting camera instruction manual
Keys to unlock the padlock used to secure the unit
Compass for north or south orientation
Pocket knife for opening battery packs
Lens cleaner and cloth for the camera and monitor
Handsaw and pruning shears
Rubber gloves for handling unit
Scent killer spray
Pen and note pad for documenting setup or anything important

Each unit should be checked to ensure it is functioning properly. Set all of the cameras to record the date and time each image is captured, and set all of them on a ten-minute delay to avoid shooting all of the film or using up the flash memory card on just a few deer. McKinley, who has captured well over fifty thousand images with scouting cameras, refers to deer that burn up his images at bait locations as "corn junkies," and we can learn from his extensive experience.

Once the scouting cameras are all set up and secure, pre-bait the area for a minimum of five days. Check the baiting laws in your state or province before beginning. If there is any confusion, contact the local conservation officer and make him aware of what you are planning to do before you start.

Do not turn the scouting cameras on during the pre-baiting period, because it is advisable to get the location established before beginning the actual survey.

McKinley suggests an effective approach that he uses in pre-baiting: place approximately fifteen pounds of corn twelve feet from the camera's lens. This

10/18/06 1:02 AM

Too much corn can cause the bait to spoil. Use approximately fifteen pounds.

small amount is to avoid aflatoxin, which can happen if the corn gets wet and sits out long enough for mold to start forming. Check the pre-bait every other day for verification of deer use. Wait for the deer to clean up the pre-baited corn before baiting again and beginning the actual survey.

Although some research has shown that shorter survey periods of five to ten days can be just as precise for sex-ratio and age structure information, McKinley and Snavely both prefer ten- to fourteen-day survey durations to maximize the density estimates and to provide more time for bashful deer to show up in front of the camera's lens. They referenced the research study led by Dr. Harry Jacobson, which sought to determine the accuracy of three camera densities by surveying a whitetail deer population that was collared with different colors for individual identification. The survey lasted a total of fourteen days, and during the first year of the two-year research study they recaptured thirty of thirty, or 100 percent of the deer, on images using a scouting camera density of one per 160 acres. McKinley captured almost the identical percentages on a similar study. Although he was capturing new bucks on days thirteen and fourteen, he believes that over 90 percent of what is captured in a fourteen-day survey can be captured in ten days. He was only picking up one or two new bucks after the tenth day of a survey, but for optimal survey results fourteen days is what biologists should be using in the field for their research.

When the fourteen-day survey is completed, compile all the images and vigilantly count the number of bucks, does, and fawns. Don't concern yourself if you guess that you are counting the same does and fawns more than once. Total up all the does and fawns, including the known repeats. On the bucks, tally up two numbers: the total number of bucks in the images including the repeats, and the actual number of unique bucks. To clarify, if fifty images of total bucks were captured in the survey, and twenty are easily recognizable bucks, when counting the number of the unique bucks simply use different antler characteristics, such as number of points, spread, abnormal points, tine length, or overall mass.

In most instances there will be a few deer that are unidentifiable. Merely throw those deer out of the survey equation. Don't make a guess on any deer out of the flash range of the scouting camera.

It is quite simple to identify the number of bucks with unique antler characteristics; on the other hand, does and fawns really have no distinguishable characteristics that let them be counted individually. To separate the number of individual does and fawns from the repeats, a population factor must be computed into the figures. Just take the number of unique bucks (20) and divide this by the total number of buck images (50). The resulting population factor ($20 \div 50 = 0.40$) is then multiplied by the number of does and fawns counted in the images. If the total was, say, 100 does and fawns in the images, multiplying by the population factor of 0.40 gives an estimate of 40 individual does.

The population factor filters out all those corn junkies that come to the baited scouting camera locations multiple times. In other words, by using the known number of bucks that revisit the scouting camera location it can be determined how many of the does and fawns are repeats. This obviously assumes that the bucks and does are just as likely to visit the scouting camera locations. In McKinley's study, individually tagged does were used to establish if bucks and does visited the scouting camera locations at the same rate. From this study he established no noteworthy difference in usage rates.

Once the total population has been estimated it is possible to compute a buck-to-doe ratio, and fawn-to-doe ratio. This requires a developed ability for aging the bucks on the parcel of property. They should be sorted by age class so the age structure can be examined. As the survey process is repeated over multiple seasons it will be possible to compare trends in the estimates. In fact, season-to-season trends in this type of information are much more significant than the actual population estimates in any particular year.

McKinley's research in Mississippi, where late fawning commonly occurs, showed that the most accurate fawn crop estimates are derived from a post-hunting season or winter survey, because fawns don't move around a lot during the fall survey periods. The older northern fawns could be much more active than their later-born relatives from the South. In the North, because of the climate, fawns must reach a significant body weight of roughly sixty pounds before the unsympathetic winter weather sets in. More research must be conducted in the North to determine if this is the case in the colder climates with lingering winters. The best thing about scouting camera technology is that anyone can become a researcher or scientist just by purchasing several units and using them in the deer woods. Conduct a study comparing the fawn crop results from the fall and winter surveys. Collect observation data on the number of fawns observed per doe to have another piece of information gleaned from the study.

It doesn't matter if hunters have one hundred or ten thousand acres of property to work with or they just want to take pictures of deer, scouting cameras will become one of their most cherished belongings. These surveys may not answer every question on deer management; however, they are enjoyable to conduct and limited only by your imagination. The bonus of a scouting camera survey is the photos of deer on a property that can be kept for enjoyment.

How to Conduct a Scouting Camera Survey

1. Depending on the desired accuracy, grid the property into one-hundred or two hundred-acre compartments. Locate a bait site with high deer use near the center of each compartment if possible, and clear vegetation and branches within a ten-foot radius.

2. Select a tree or install a post twelve to fifteen feet from the center of the circle and set the scouting camera unit facing either north or south to avoid sun glare. Pay special attention to the "view" of the camera and remove any obstructions. A numbered sign in the view identifies the site.

3. Pre-bait each site for five days with fifteen pounds of corn in the center of the circle and check daily. Notify the local Conservation Officer that a deer survey is being conducted.

4. Set the camera to record the date and time with a ten-minute delay between pictures.

5. Set the monitor so the beam is aimed twenty-four to thirty inches above the bait to eliminate unwanted images of raccoons and other small animals.

6. Operate cameras for five to fourteen days, depending on your budget and desired accuracy. Check cameras daily if possible, replacing film or memory cards as needed. Use 200 ASA print film with 36 exposures or 1GB Flash Card memory to achieve the most images of deer activity.

7. Analyze the images to determine total number of images each of bucks, does, and fawns and number of individual bucks. Do not include unidentifiable deer.

Sample Survey Calculations
Acres Surveyed = 1,000
Scouting Camera Sites = 10 with 1 scouting camera per 100 acres
Consecutive Survey Days = 7
Total Photographs of Deer = 490

Buck Photos = 120 (individual bucks identified = 35)
Doe Photos = 230
Fawn Photos = 140

8. Use the relationship of the number of unique bucks (35) to the total number of bucks photographed (120) to calculate a population factor.
   35/120 = .29

Research has concluded 80 percent of the deer are photographed after 7 days, so adjust by an extrapolation factor of 1/.8 = 1.25.

Estimates of Population Characteristics

Bucks		$35 \times 1.25 = 44$
Does	$230 \times .29 =$	$67 \times 1.25 = 84$
Fawns	$140 \times .29 =$	$41 \times 1.25 = 51$

Total Population = 179

Results

Acres Per Deer = 1,000/179 = 5.6
Buck-to-Doe Ratio = 35:67 = 1:19
Fawn Crop = fawn/doe = 41/67 = .61 or 61%

I would like to thank the following for their help compiling this research data into a format that anyone can use to conduct a formal infrared-triggered scouting camera deer survey, similar to what professional researchers have been doing for years.

William McKinley, Whitetail Deer Project Leader, State of Mississippi
Dr. Stephen Demarais, Professor, Mississippi State University
Jason Snavely, President, Drop-Tine Wildlife Consulting
Dr. Harry Jacobson, Professor Emeritus, Mississippi State University, Wildlife Consultant

CHAPTER 13

Designing a QDM Strategy Using Your Scouting Camera

Perhaps the single most effective way of growing big bucks on your property is to practice Quality Deer Management (QDM). Your scouting camera will help you to determine how best to implement this strategy on a parcel of property, but first everyone needs to understand what QDM is.

QDM is a management philosophy or practice that unites landowners, hunters, and managers in a common goal of producing biologically and socially balanced deer herds within existing environments, while respecting social and legal constraints. This approach typically involves the protection of young bucks (yearlings and some 2½ year olds) combined with an adequate harvest of does to maintain a healthy population in balance with existing habitat conditions and landowner desires. This level of deer management involves the production of quality deer (bucks, does, and fawns), quality habitat, quality hunting experiences, and most importantly, quality hunters.

A successful QDM program requires an increased knowledge of deer biology and active participation in management. This level of involvement extends the role of the hunter from mere consumer to manager. The progression from education to understanding and finally to respect, bestows an ethical obligation upon the hunter to practice sound deer management. Consequently, to an increasing number of landowners and hunters, QDM is a desirable alternative to traditional management, which allows the harvest of any legal buck and few, if any, does.

QDM guidelines are formulated according to property-specific objectives, goals, and limitations. Participating hunters enjoy both the tangible and intangible benefits of the approach. Pleasure can be derived from each hunting experience regardless of whether or not a shot is fired. What is most important is the chance to harvest a quality buck—an opportunity lacking in many areas under traditional management practices. When a quality buck is taken on a QDM area, the pride can be shared by all property hunters because it was they who allowed the buck to reach an older age class, which is necessary for large bodies and antlers.

Texas is the formal birthplace of QDM. Two early pioneers, Al Brothers and Murphy E. Ray Jr. originally popularized this novel concept in their 1975 book, *Producing Quality Whitetails.* This idea was brought to the Southeast in the late 1970s and it has been employed successfully on millions of acres of private and public lands throughout the entire United States.

THE FOUR BUILDING BLOCKS OF QUALITY DEER MANAGEMENT

While QDM guidelines must be tailored to each property, there are four corner-stones to all successful QDM programs: herd management, habitat management, hunter management, and herd monitoring.

Herd Management

Arguably, the most important part of QDM is herd management. Determining the appropriate number of deer to harvest by sex and age is essential. The first step is to establish the number of deer the habitat can support in a healthy condition. Thus, habitat quality determines herd size, herd quality, and harvest requirements for both sexes.

It is often difficult to establish the appropriate herd size for a property because it is not a fixed value from year to year, or even season to season. Habitats are constantly changing and seasonal conditions vary. Land use changes on the property or adjacent properties also affect habitat quality. However, with a little homework and some advice from a wildlife professional, a reasonable starting point can be established.

The manager must understand that deer health will decline if it exceeds the habitat's capacity to provide quality forage and cover. A good indication of habitat quality is deer body weights, especially in young deer. A decrease in average body weight within an age class often indicates a decrease in habitat quality. In bucks, an average antler measurement within an age class also provides useful insight regarding current habitat quality. With does, other warning signs include a reduction in the average number of fawns per doe or the lactation rate in adult does.

Habitat Management

Improving the nutrition available to a deer herd is another important component of QDM. The diet of a healthy herd should contain 12 to 18 percent protein and adequate levels of calcium, phosphorous, and other important nutrients. Although whitetails can maintain themselves on lower-quality diets, antler development, body growth, and reproductive success suffer. Fortunately, several techniques are available to increase nutrition to desirable levels. Three common practices include natural vegetation management, food plots, and supplemental feeding.

Hunter Management

The management of hunters is a critical component, yet very often a difficult aspect of any QDM program. Within most hunting groups, support for QDM varies, sometimes even substantially. It is difficult to achieve the objectives of QDM unless all hunters are fully committed. Education is the key. Hunters must fully understand the benefits and costs of QDM before they become active participants.

Active participation in a QDM program requires hunters to learn about ecology and behavior, and become participants in management. They must be able to distinguish fawns, does, yearling bucks, intermediate-aged bucks ($2^1/2$ and $3^1/2$ years old) and mature bucks ($4^1/2$ years and older). Making these distinctions requires knowledge of body size, shape, behavior, and other features related to sex and age. Again, education is the key to success.

Knowledge leads to increased respect for the quarry and often a greater focus on the experience rather than the number or size of the animals harvested. Conversations with other hunters become focused on what is observed and left rather than what is taken. Landowners and clubs can become better neighbors as they unite to have areas large enough for QDM. In brief, QDM fosters a sense of pride in the deer herd and nature as a whole.

Herd Monitoring

Herd monitoring is the last building block of QDM. There are two types of data commonly collected: harvest data and observation data. Harvest data should be collected from deer harvested during the season or found dead at other times.

10/27/06 12:26 PM   Brad Hansmann   *Cuddeback*

Participants in a QDM program must be able to distinguish between a $1^1/2$- year-old deer like this one and more mature bucks.

Observation data may be collected by hunters or with scouting cameras. Scouting cameras have the advantage that they can monitor deer at night and when no one is hunting the area, as well as provide useful reference photographs. This is especially important for mature bucks, which are infrequently seen by hunters except during the rut. The photographs taken can provide useful information on herd size, sex ratio, and buck abundance and age structure. They also can raise the excitement level around the deer camp and verify that management efforts to produce older bucks are working. Together, this data helps hunters and managers make educated decisions about their deer herds. Good records generally result in good management decisions, whereas poor or incomplete records often result in faulty decisions.

It takes a substantial amount of data to develop a good picture of a herd. On many properties, the number of deer taken is too small and measurements are too variable for conclusions to be drawn from a single year's data. Therefore data must be collected over several years or combined with surrounding properties data to determine trends in herd condition.

Increasingly, landowners, hunters, and wildlife managers across North America are embracing the QDM philosophy. This is evidenced by the increasing voluntary and regulatory implementation of QDM practices on private and public lands. Hunters are rethinking what constitutes a quality hunt and how they can make a positive contribution to the future of the deer herds they hunt.

Another benefit of QDM is increased hunter safety. By taking the time to positively identify each deer by sex and age, the likelihood of accidental shootings is even more remote than under current management methods. Hunters participating in QDM enjoy the tangible and intangible benefits of this approach. What is important is the chance to interact with a well-managed deer herd that is in balance with its habitat.

The Quality Deer Management Association has an informative web site at www.QDMA.com.

RESEARCH WITH SCOUTING CAMERAS
It has been almost twenty years since these neat little surveillance tools made their appearance, and some of the country's leading whitetail deer researchers have dramatically refined their use. We can learn a lot from these professionals that will help determine how best to implement the finest QDM strategy on our own parcel of property. Researchers working with major universities and the QDMA (Quality Deer Management Association) are continually coming up with new material that will enhance a program to produce quality whitetail deer.

Age Structures and Harvest Quota
Dr. Harry Jacobson conducted the ground-breaking research study using scouting cameras to conduct deer surveys in 1997. Since that time, he has conducted

extensive research on his survey techniques in many locations of the country. He has determined that scouting camera surveys are not restricted to a deer census. In addition to a census, it is possible to determine the age structures of the bucks along with a harvest quota by age class. Individual bucks can be identified that can be either included in a planned harvest or protected from the harvest. Also, identifying the general condition of the herd or presence of diseased or injured animals can be achieved by reviewing the images captured. In addition, surveys allow the measurement of the QDM management progress for antler qualities, sex ratios, fawn crop, and the age structure of the bucks from one year to the next.

Patterns of Deer Activity

Dr. James Knoll, Director for the Institute for Whitetail Deer Management and Research in Texas and one of the nation's most respected researchers on whitetail deer, has been able to determine daily patterns of deer activity using scouting cameras. He believes with the use of these effective observation tools it is possible to determine to a great extent daily activity patterns, and how deer might be affected by the phase of the moon and its position, time of year, weather conditions, and hunting pressure. He has found that deer have identical pre-dawn, midday, and late-evening activity peaks under all phases of the moon or geographic location; however, the extent of activity peaks can be affected by a variety of environmental and human-caused factors. Comparisons of activity patterns for deer that were hunted and those that were not hunted indicated adult bucks have a tendency to develop into increasingly nocturnal animals, and this trend seems to be more genetic than learned. Knoll has also used scouting cameras to determine the phenology of buck antler development and breeding. If the deer herd is monitored from midsummer through late winter, it is possible to establish the yearly period of shedding velvet, when rubs and scrapes are established, locations of staging areas and sanctuaries, establishment of buck bachelor groups and their breakup, the breeding cycle, and the timing of the shedding of antlers.

Mock Scrapes

Ben Koerth conducted a five-year research study in Texas at the Institute for Whitetail Deer Management and Research using scouting cameras to determine if they would capture fewer images of non-target species at mock scrapes versus baits. In the first three years he used commercial deer scents applied to mock scrapes using dominant buck urine, doe-in-estrus urine, and combinations of urines. He also laid scent lines along trails. All of the locations were visited by deer, but the mock scrapes combined with the urine scents had the most visits. It was clear that the olfactory cue combined with the visual cue attracted deer more often. He was unable to determine with certainty whether the deer were

Mock scrapes reduce the number of photos of non-target species.

10/18/06 6:36 PM   Anderson

One of the problems with using a bait pile is that bait attracts more than just deer.

12/28/06 3:40 AM   Robert Davis

attracted to the scents used in the mock scrapes mainly as a sexual attractant or if they were just curious. Using attractant scents combined with a mock scrape reduced the number of non-target images considerably. Over the entire study period, the bulk of deer that were captured on images at mock scrapes were bucks. Also, using mock scrapes with attractant scents appeared to capture an impartial sample of all ages of bucks. It was determined from the study that using attractant scents in mock scrapes could be a useful technique to record the buck segment of a deer herd with fewer non-target species images.

Large Deer Survey

The QDMA management team performed what is likely the largest scouting camera survey ever conducted, on a twelve-thousand-acre lease in Kentucky. Conducting an accurate deer survey using infrared-triggered scouting cameras on a parcel that large is an enormous task. QDMA Heartland Regional Director and Wildlife Biologist Chris Pevey set up and ran the survey with help from the people leasing the property. They ran a ten-day survey with forty scouting cameras on half the property and then moved the scouting cameras to the other half and conducted another ten-day survey. Each site was pre-baited with corn, mineral blocks, and a mineral attractant mix. Halfway through the survey period, all the memory cards in the digital cameras needed to be changed because so many images were being captured. Every one of the scouting camera units were set on a ten-minute delay and still every unit averaged 425 to 450 images during the course of the ten-day survey.

Pevey used BuckSpy Advanced software to sort and categorize all the images and produce the final data, but first he had to identify each deer by its sex, age, and (for bucks) antler size.

The company leasing the property had hunters coming in for bow season and they wanted to determine how many bucks were $2^1/2$ years old or older or that would score at least 140 or better. Pevey pulled all the images of bucks meeting that criteria on each scouting camera from the first half of the property survey, and it totaled thirty-five individual shooter bucks.

The personnel leasing the property took the images and put together a booklet of all the shooter bucks to show the bow hunters coming in the area. They also put together another booklet with images of bucks that were off limits because they had great potential as future trophies.

When Pevey started to review the images from the second half of the property, which was the side of the property with the most agriculture, he discovered even better bucks. He also noticed some neat genetic trends in the images of the bucks' antlers. About 30 percent of the mature bucks had matching kickers off the back of their G2s. He also noticed that the mature bucks were captured at different locations more often than the immature bucks.

This deer survey was an incredible amount of work, but the knowledge gained far outweighed the effort. Hunters could actually see what the standards were for the property and as a result many hunters passed on respectable bucks in order to better manage the herd.

Feed Evaluation

Cristy G. Brown an instructor in Wildlife Science, Tarleton State University in Stephenville, Texas, conducted a research study using scouting cameras to determine if supplemental feeding actually reaches the species of interest. Millions of dollars are spent each year on supplemental feeding programs for whitetail deer, and this study set out to determine the success of supplemental feeding programs.

The study concluded that the use of scouting cameras will help a supplemental feeding program be cost-effective. It will also provide important information about the feeding habits of the whitetail deer on a property.

ESTIMATING AGE OF DEER

The ability to accurately estimate the age of live wild deer is a priceless skill for anyone managing a parcel of property. Scouting cameras provide a tremendous opportunity to practice and learn this skill. Accurately assigning bucks into age groups is an essential part of assessing the improvement of the QDM program. I have been estimating the age, antler score, weight, and health of whitetail deer since I was a young man and I still disagree with other professional deer mangers. Keep in mind that aging a whitetail deer on the hoof is not exact science; even the experts will disagree. Throw in other variables like geographic location—deer are much larger in the North than the South—and you can see why it can be so difficult. The key is to practice evaluating images from scouting cameras, and over time the skill will develop. Pinpointing the age of a buck $3^1/2$ years or older is extremely complex, but for practical purposes, categorizing bucks into $1^1/2$, $2^1/2$, and $3^1/2+$ age groups will be adequate.

Because determining the age of wild deer is not always clear, frequently it takes input from several reviewers to reach a consensus on the age of a deer. Additionally, a reviewer that is outvoted from a panel after reviewing the image is not always incorrect. Aging wild bucks from images requires the consideration of many factors. Decisions must be based on the prevalence of proof. Because whitetail deer across the North American range vary so much in size and shape, it is best to gather as much data as possible about the deer from the area to improve the accuracy of estimating the age of the deer.

Start by gathering as much information as possible on bucks that are harvested during the hunting season. This should include the girth of the neck, chest, and stomach along with measurements of the antlers like beam length and mass. Then compare this information with the buck's age based on the jawbone. Over time this will develop an age class standard for the physical parameters of the deer from that area. Also refer back to all the images of the bucks that were harvested once the jawbone age has been determined. This will help hone the skill of aging a deer when looking at future images of live bucks.

FEED EVALUATION

By using the correct experimental design, scouting cameras can aid in evaluating efficient placement of supplemental feeders, determine the success of different feeds, and give the owner of the property evidence of deer frequenting a parcel of property. Start by using a map of the property to determine the different habitat types (planted food plots, lowlands, and uplands, etc.). This will establish where the scouting cameras/feed sites should be positioned. Each one of the habitat types should have equal representation to best represent the parcel of property.

When evaluating the diverse feed types it is essential to have a group of feed sites at each random point within that type of habitat. The group should include the substitute feeds being evaluated and a control feed, which is usually whole corn. Set the scouting cameras on ten-minute intervals to avoid getting duplicate images. The first image from each location on the scouting camera should have the site number. This can be accomplished by painting a number on the feeder or putting a stake in the ground on a food plot with a number. This will match the appropriate feed site location to the image for future reference. The scouting cameras should be operational for at least fourteen days and should be checked every few days, whether a film or a digital scouting camera is used. After reviewing the images, the results will need to be analyzed to determine which feeder locations were the most successful and whether the alternative feed was more effective than the controlled feed at each location. This method of using scouting cameras will assist in making supplemental feeding programs much more cost-effective and provide important information about the feeding habits of whitetail deer.

HUNTING SHED ANTLERS

Several friends and I have used scouting cameras to monitor bucks shedding their antlers. We begin our search for the shed antlers as soon as most of the images show the bucks have dropped their racks. In most regions, rodents will immediately begin chewing on the antlers as soon as they hit the ground, and we want to beat them to the racks. Keep in mind that the timing of the bucks shedding their antlers varies geographically.

We concentrate our search for the shed antlers in the places that have produced the best for us in past seasons:

Winter food sources, especially late-season food plots in regions without deep snow depths

Bedding areas or thick winter cover

In bottlenecks that link the bedding and feeding areas together

Near a water source, especially if water is limited on the property

Where deer must jump along travel routes like fences, ditches, and creeks

Brushy areas along travel routes—in these areas sheds may even be found above the ground

Then we rank them from where the most were found to where the least were found. Always walk very slowly, constantly scanning the ground downrange but also concentrating close to your feet. Although some sheds will be immediately noticeable, most are spotted within one or two steps of the trail. Try not to be distracted by the surroundings, but if it happens, slow down and remember to keep your eyes on the ground close to your feet. Ovals in the snow up north or in bedding areas where the bucks bed down can signal an increased chance of finding a matched set of antlers.

Hunting for shed antlers can be extremely rewarding and fun for the entire family. So don't put away your scouting cameras after the hunting season. Keep them out and hunt for some monster sheds.

CONCLUSION

Historically, biologists and deer project leaders have concentrated their efforts on increasing whitetail deer populations in a state or property by shielding antlerless deer from being harvested. This approach has dramatically increased our whitetail deer population across the entire North American range from the all-time lows of the early 1900s to the record amount of animals we have today. In fact, they are overpopulated in many areas, causing new problems for deer managers to overcome. Progressive deer managers of today are concentrating their efforts on improving the quality of the herd where the deer populations are well established.

QDM is an approach and philosophy that involves managing whitetail deer in a biologically and generally sound manner within the existing habitat conditions. QDM is not trophy deer management like many people believe, where all importance is placed on producing bucks with monster racks, and it is not about just shooting the does of the herd. Every state or parcel of property has its own restrictions from the genetic structure of the deer herd, to its soil fertility, to land use practices and more. The people interested in better managing the deer in an area must realize these limitations and concentrate all effort into allowing the deer herd to reach its full potential without impractical expectations. Managing whitetail deer is a complex task, which is influenced by many factors, with age, nutrition, and genetics at the forefront.

Uses of scouting cameras are only restricted by a person's imagination. Just look at what researchers have accomplished over the last several years in the field. The value of these great research tools are unlimited and it's anyone's guess who will discover the next technique that will enhance our knowledge of the whitetail deer.

For more information on QDMA (Quality Deer Management Association) contact the Quality Deer Management Association by telephone at 800-209-DEER or online at www.qdma.org.

CHAPTER 14

Tracking Survey Results from Year to Year

The dynamics of your deer herd will change from year to year based on the severity of winter, other weather conditions, and its effect on food sources, disease, hunting pressure, and management practices, not to mention what's going on in neighboring properties. By comparing and analyzing your annual survey results, you can determine what actions need to be taken.

Chapter 13 discusses how to conduct a formal deer survey and distinguish individual bucks based on their antler characteristics, as well as determining how many buck, doe, and fawn images were gathered during the survey period. Also based on the total number of unique buck images captured during the survey period, a population factor is determined to convert the raw numbers of does and fawns in the herd on the property during the survey period.

After a deer survey is completed, the scouting cameras have been pulled from the property, and the images have been totally reviewed, take the survey results to the next level by estimating the bucks' ages and rough Boone and Crockett scores. One should also check the ratio of yearling spikes to yearling bucks with forked antlers, which is an indicator of the condition of the herd. Ultimately, all of the essential estimates from the survey should be logged on paper, which include deer density, adult sex ratios, estimated age structure of the bucks, estimated antler score, yearly spike ratio, and fawn crop.

Now, for all the questions that remain about what comes next:

- What should be done with this information?
- How does one begin to interpret these results from the survey?
- What do all these numbers mean about the deer herd on the property?
- What overall management decisions and actions should be taken with all data, now and in the future?

This chapter discusses how to analyze, organize, and summarize your deer survey results. Once that is complete, it will show how to connect the dots to

11/14/06   9:12 PM

The ratio of spike bucks to bucks with forked antlers is a good indicator of herd condition.

make wise management decisions with the deer herd. Scouting camera surveys can be used on the majority of properties to make sound deer management decisions on a deer herd. However, most individuals using scouting cameras do not realize all the information that can be gained from the images.

It is critical to gather this data over time before making any management decisions that will affect the herd. One or two years of survey results is not enough data to make vital management decisions. A total of three to five years is needed to isolate trends before making any sound choices affecting the deer herd.

Most landowners and hunters are usually only concerned with the number of deer that are on their parcel of property during the hunting season. This can be closely joined with the number of deer per square mile on the property. Although this information is important, it is only one piece of the large management puzzle when the survey results are compiled.

ESTIMATES OF DEER DENSITY

The density estimates resulting from a scouting camera survey identify a population limited to the study area during the time the survey was conducted. The study area could encompass two hundred or even ten thousand acres of property and free-ranging deer will be frequently crossing over boundary lines during the entire year. The home range size of the whitetail deer varies across their entire North American range during the year for many reasons, including fawning, the rut, winter conditions, age, sex, and quality and diversity of the habitat on the property. The problem is that the majority of property owners or clubs do not have power over sufficient acreage to keep the deer from traveling over the property boundaries. Some deer that are on the property will never show up in an image.

Dr. Charles DeYoung of Texas A&M University has spent a lifetime studying whitetail deer and believes they are extremely individualistic. As an example, several years ago he trapped two mature bucks that were approximately the same age and antler size. He collared both of them with telemetry units so their movements could be tracked. One of the bucks never moved from the area where he was trapped, and his total movement was only about eighty acres. The other buck, that was living under the exact conditions, regularly traveled two or three miles from his core area. The buck occasionally traveled completely out of range of the telemetry equipment. DeYoung's findings show that we must keep in mind that deer density results will only reveal a snapshot that was taken during the survey period. Before making any management decisions from the results of deer-density estimates, it is crucial to constantly evaluate trends in the data over time.

To gain insight into a deer herd it is critical to repeat scouting camera surveys on a regular basis. Methods must remain consistent every time a survey is conducted. Scouting camera locations should be recorded on a GPS unit, and every survey should last for fourteen days to ensure the maximum amounts of deer are recorded. Research has established that surveys lasting longer in duration than fourteen days are not cost-effective and will not considerably increase the accuracy of the results. It is worthwhile to create simple bar graphs of the total estimated population from all of the annual surveys using Microsoft Excel or one of the other software programs available. If the scouting camera survey methods were consistent, trends can be isolated in response to the established management program; however, there are many variables that can affect your survey results even when consistent survey methods have been maintained. Constantly be aware of this likelihood and look for assistance in interpreting the data if anything seems out of kilter.

Although the significance of the survey data lies in the trends, most biologists want to hear a target density number. It would be wise to contact the state or regional deer biologist or project leader and talk over the goals for the property, and ask him or her to assist in developing a target deer density for the region and habitat type.

ADULT BUCK-TO-DOE RATIO

There have been numerous research studies and a lot written about adult buck-to-doe ratios, with very good rationale. It is a critical gauge of the condition of a deer herd. Luckily, the adult buck-to-doe ratio is fairly simple to manage by just regulating the harvest. The deer herd is headed down the proper path

Most management programs look for a buck-to-doe ratio of approximately one to two.

as long as the anterless harvest program is improving the adult buck-to-doe ratio of the herd.

Adult buck-to-doe ratios across the entire North American range of the whitetail deer is tilted in the direction of does. Interestingly, all the research studies conducted indicate numerous negative factors that a tilted sex ratio figure can have on a population of deer. These negative factors include lengthened fawning and breeding periods, increased post-rut, mortality of bucks, decreased rivalry for does during the duration of the rut, and amplified rut-related strain on immature bucks. The adult buck-to-doe ratio is managed with the property owner's preferred population composition goal in mind. These goals are tremendously varied, but most management programs should aspire for one adult buck for every one to two adult does in the population. This goal can only be achieved by a control in harvesting the immature bucks and a moderate to aggressive harvest of the does in the population. In just a few years of collecting data and adjusting the harvest, trends will be noticed. Some researchers even suggest maintaining a bar graph with a quality zone at a buck-to-doe ratio of 1:1.5.

These research studies indicate why it is critical to monitor trends over time before making management decisions on harvests. They also suggest taking care not to over-harvest does on a property, because they are completely devoted to the location where they were born. One study found that 80 percent of bucks dispersed more than two miles from where they were born and several dispersed as far as twenty-five miles. This suggests that if the bucks were literally hunted out of an area, more bucks would ultimately show up to fill the empty space. On the other hand, if the does were hunted out of the area it would be a long time before the void was filled by another doe moving into the area.

10/12/06 2:42 AM   Greg Hamilton   Cuddeback

One study found that 80 percent of bucks disperse more than two miles from where they were born.

Research has also proven that pressure from the doe is what causes a year-ling buck to disperse from his home range. It had been previously believed that younger bucks dispersed because of social pressure they received from the mature dominant bucks. In a study, leading whitetail deer researcher Dr. Larry Marchinton deliberately orphaned fifteen fawn bucks shortly after being weaned. He also tracked nineteen bucks that grew up under their doe mothers. When the bucks reached $2\frac{1}{2}$ years of age, 87 percent of the bucks with surviving mothers had dispersed, but only 9 percent of the bucks that were orphaned had dispersed from their home range.

BUCKS WITH UNIQUE CHARACTERISTICS

Using a graph to log the number of individual bucks over $1\frac{1}{2}$ years of age captured on an image during an annual scouting camera survey serves as an excellent gauge when assessing the ability to protect these immature bucks from the fall hunting harvest. It is vital to provide safe cover and sanctuaries for the young to middle-aged bucks in the herd within the property boundaries during the hunting season to capitalize on the number that will reach the mature age class. Some will be lost to herd dynamics, such as being hit by a vehicle, shot on the neighbor's property, or lost to a buck fight. To minimize the extent to which this affects the overall management program on the property, focus on a very detailed plan on how the property is laid out. Accomplishing the goals in any management program is dependent on the ability to shield immature bucks from being prematurely killed. If the buck harvest on the property is restricted to only mature bucks the number of mature bucks will increase over time. The young bucks make up the bulk of the buck population. By not harvesting these younger age classes they are better able to survive and move up into the older

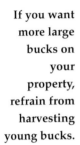

If you want more large bucks on your property, refrain from harvesting young bucks.

10/10/06 5:11 AM   Tim Simmons

brackets resulting in more mature bucks, with better chances of having trophy racks on the top of their heads.

FAWN RECRUITMENT

This is somewhat different than fawn crop, which means the total number of fawns actually born. The majority of biologists refer to fawn recruitment as the total number of fawns that live to their first hunting season. The key is to get them to the fall population so they can be considered an addition to the herd. Fawn recruitment is by far one of the best indicators of the deer herd condition in relationship to habitat quality. Extensive research studies have recognized a very strong connection between the quality of the habitat and deer density relative to fawn recruitment. When the population of deer on a property increases beyond the carrying capacity of the habitat, the number of fawns recruited annually decreases. On the other hand, with a lower-density herd, population with high-quality feed is abundant, and twin fawns will be the rule. Under those ideal conditions many yearling does and even some fawn does will have fawns. But when the deer density increases, so does the competition for quality food, causing fewer adult does to give birth to twin fawns. Additionally, many of the yearling does and all fawn does will fail to produce fawns.

When graphing fawn recruitment, use a quality zone that represents a goal for the particular management plan for the property. Just like deer density and buck-to-doe ratios, this number will fluctuate dramatically across the entire whitetail range. Most deer managers will try for a fawn recruitment of at least 0.75 fawns that live to the opening day of deer season for each adult doe in the population.

Tracking buck age structure and yearling spike ratios is helpful for sound herd management.

10/10/06   7:20 AM

BUCK FACTORS

It is especially helpful to track the buck age structure estimates along with the yearling spike ratios on the property. Hunter expectations differ enormously, but typically quality hunts flourish when at least 30 percent of the adult buck population over $1^1/_2$ years old is $3^1/_2$ years of age and older. Roughly 15 percent of the bucks in the $4^1/_2+$ age range is optimal.

Obtain the yearling spike ratio by dividing the number of spike-antlered yearling bucks by the total number of spike and branch-antlered yearling bucks combined. Even under good management, the percent of spike-antlered yearling bucks in a given population varies significantly. Seek professional advice from an experienced deer biologist in the local area to determine what a realistic goal for the property should be.

Scouting cameras can be used to collect a lot of data from a deer survey. Compiling all the data can be educational and great fun. The key to the management program on any parcel of property lies in putting it all together so the puzzle doesn't have any pieces missing. Carefully examine every image for every category, and seek help from the state professional biologist if needed. Make sure to isolate trends over time before making any management decisions that will affect the deer herd. Once management decisions have been implemented it is critical to graph the trends so tweaks or changes can be made immediately if needed.

Contact Information: Quality Deer Management Association, 800-209-DEER, www.qdma.com
Drop-Tine Wildlife Consulting
Jason Snavely
570-458-0477

PART FOUR

CHAPTER 15

Using Your Scouting Camera to Hunt Bear and Other Game

SCOUTING FOR BEARS

Bear hunters find a scouting camera particularly useful at bait stations. Not only will the scouting camera tell the hunter when the bears are hitting the baits, it will show the size of bears that are coming to the bait. The scouting camera will tell the hunter which baits have the best potential for drawing both quantities of bears as well as those with the best trophy potential. The one possible drawback connected with using scouting cameras for bears is the bears' penchant for destroying scouting cameras placed at bait stations. Read on to learn how to reduce the likelihood of this happening to your scouting camera.

How to Know What Bears Are Hitting the Bait

There are many ways to determine size, color phase, and the numbers of bears that are hitting a bait station. Back thirty years ago when I was guiding, we had to read the sign in the area. We really had no way of knowing for sure how many or what sizes of bears were hitting the baits. We could look for tracks and hair to estimate size and determine if we had a color phase bear coming into our baits. Then technology gave us the trail timer. This little unit placed at a bait station would give the time an animal came to the bait, but it wouldn't tell us if it was a bear. It could have been anything from a raccoon to a coyote. It was a guessing game trying to determine when they were visiting the baits. Today, technology has improved upon conjecture and supposition, and the most accurate way of determining what the animals visiting a bait site are, and what they are up to, is by using a scouting camera. A scouting camera can also give you the times that bears are visiting the bait station, which is invaluable data to your hunting strategy. A hunter can read the sign that will be available at the bait like scat, hair, and maybe even a clear print of a track. The diameter of the scat is an indicator of size. The larger the diameter of the scat, the bigger the bear. While a bear is working the bait drum, especially around the hole in the drum, hair will be pulled out as he reaches into the drum; this will show the color of the bear.

5/15/06 4:49 AM   Pat Gauthier   *Cuddeback*

Scouting camera photos allow you to assess the size of the bear hitting a bait.

5/28/06 8:05 PM   Pat Gauthier   *Cuddeback*

Before scouting cameras, it was difficult to determine how many bears were hitting the bait.

Many times a clear print of the front paw can be found near the drum in the area that was cleared. These are all good indicators and can help the hunter make a reasonable deduction, but nothing is as accurate as looking at pictures of bears hitting the bait with the exact time they were there.

I have had great results scouting bears using the Cuddeback Digital Scouting Camera over the last couple of years, especially the NoFlash model. Cuddeback also manufactures a great enclosure for cameras called a BearSafe. This unit is a completely enclosed metal box, laser-cut and powder-coated, that will ensure the

A color phase bear is easy to find with a camera; before scouting cameras, guides would look for a single hair on a bait barrel.

Bears will ruin your scouting camera if it is not protected. This is a Cuddeback Bear Safe.

scouting camera will not be bitten and destroyed by a curious bear. It can also be secured and locked to a tree and theft will be very difficult.

When setting up the scouting camera, use the bait drum as a reference point. This will ensure something beside the bear is in the frame of the picture. This will give the hunter something to judge the size of the bear against. I have seen many people set up their scouting cameras on one of the trails leading to the bait drum. Many times they miss a picture of the biggest bear hitting the bait because he uses a different trail all the time when entering the bait. Also, when

6/01/07   2:57 PM

Having your bait barrel in the photo gives you a reference for gauging size.

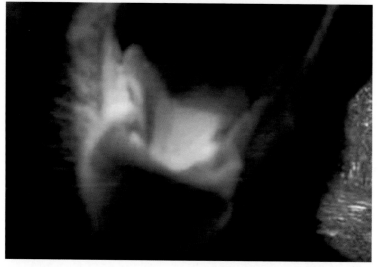

Smaller bears may bite your camera out of frustration.

small bears are entering the bait location on these trails, many times they will circle the bait to ensure "Mister Big" is not around before entering the bait. The mature bears can get very possessive of their feed source and chase off all other bears. Immature bears are totally aware of that and are very cautious. Because of this, immature bears really take their time entering the bait. In addition, if they smell the plastic from the scouting camera enclosure on the trail they will bite it out of frustration, destroying the unit if it is not in a BearSafe container.

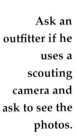

Ask an outfitter if he uses a scouting camera and ask to see the photos.

The person who is baiting should not be the one setting up the scouting camera because the bears will recognize his scent. He may also have the odor of bait on his hands and body, which could attract a bear to the scouting camera.

I remember several years ago getting some pictures on my DeerCam scouting camera that were totally black, and I thought something was wrong with the unit. Upon close examination of the pictures I realized it was a bear that must have lain down very close to the camera and taken a nap. I had the unit set up on a tree as the trail opened up to the bait barrel. Because the cover was very thick on both sides of the trail the bear must have felt very secure there and just lay down in front of the lens of the camera.

The exciting part of using scouting cameras is seeing a picture of a monster bear that you didn't know was in the area. These are the types of things that help a bear hunter stay more alert and on stand longer without getting bored. A scouting camera is a great tool for the bear hunter to add to his bag of tricks and have a lot of fun with all year long.

If I'm going on a bear hunt now I always ask outfitters if they are using scouting cameras in their program. If not, I explain to them the many benefits of using them in their operation and how cameras can help them. They can even use the pictures to get potential clients to sign up after seeing the many pictures they have of bears. It can be a great selling point because the hunter can actually see the bears that are working the outfitter's baits. Like the old saying goes, seeing is believing. This type of data just adds credibility to the outfitter. I have even gone as far as sending the outfitter a scouting camera and a BearSafe to use on potential baits that I would be hunting when I got there to determine what was hitting them before I arrived for the hunt.

Just last year I was on a spring bear hunt at Golden Eagle Lodge in northern Manitoba. The lodge is an isolated fly-in about thirty air miles northwest of the town of Lynn Lake in the remote Canadian bush. The Lynn Lake area is known to produce big bears because of the lack of hunting pressure, and I was really excited about this hunt. Golden Eagle Lodge is a hunting lodge that takes just a few bear hunters every spring. They only had three hunters in camp over the last several years. I knew this was the kind of place that could really produce a few monster bears, and I wanted to take every advantage I could because I only had a limited time to hunt.

I made arrangements with the camp manager to put out a few Cuddeback NoFlash scouting cameras on a few baits that he thought had the best potential for a big bear. When I arrived in camp we reviewed the digital images he had taken of several bears and one was indeed a world-class animal. I hunted that bait for the entire hunt and passed up several really nice bears, including a nice blonde color phase bear that had a pumpkin head, which I estimated would score very close or just over twenty inches. On the last night of the hunt the big bruin waltzed into the bait like he owned it and I was amazed at the size of this animal. I have hunted bears for almost forty years and been fortunate enough to study, guide, and harvest some great animals, but this bear was one of the biggest animals I had ever seen in the wild.

I waited for the right opportunity to make a good killing shot, drew my Mathews, and released my arrow. I knew it was a great shot as I watched the orange Blazer vanes disappear through his rib cage. He bolted into the cover behind the bait, and I heard him expire and hit the ground in the thick cover less than thirty yards behind the bait.

This is the largest bear Dick has ever shot, and he credits his scouting camera for the opportunity.

This was the first time in my life the closer I got to the animal the bigger he looked. Usually they get some sort of ground shrinkage the closer you get to the animal. He was the biggest bear I have ever harvested. We estimated he was at least fifteen years old and had an absolutely huge head with a hide that measured over 7½ feet nose to tail. After the sixty day drying period we measured the skull, and it was a whopping 22⅛ inches. He created a memory I will not forget for the rest of my life.

The moral of this story is that without the scouting camera, I never would have known for sure this bear was hitting this bait. There were several other good mature bears hitting the bait, including the large blonde color phase bear that I would have probably harvested if I hadn't known that monster was there. I never would have had an opportunity at the bear of a lifetime without those scouting cameras.

SCOUTING CAMERA SETUP TIPS FOR HUNTING BEARS

- Use a tree that is not facing into the rising or setting sun to mount the scouting camera.
- Don't attach the scouting camera to a small tree that will move in the wind. A tree that is a minimum of seven inches in diameter is best.
- Clear any weeds or branches with leaves blocking the lens of the camera so pictures are not taken of them swaying in the breeze.
- Mount the unit approximately twelve feet from the bait barrel, and never beyond forty feet. This will ensure the hunter will be able to determine the quality of bears hitting the bait. The top of the unit should be mounted to a tree three-and-a-half feet from ground level. Spray the

The optimal distance from camera to bear is twelve feet. Too much farther away will result in a difficult-to-discern image.

Cuddeback Digital Camera 5/27/07 1:39 AM Holman

entire enclosure with Scent Killer, covering the lens opening with your rubber gloves.

- I advise buying a scouting camera that has a totally enclosed locking device like the BearSafe from Cuddeback. Without this protection, it is too easy for a bear to bite the camera and destroy the unit. This happens many times when bait scent gets on the camera housing from the person setting it up not being totally scent-conscious. The bears think there is a treat inside and destroy the unit trying to get it out.

- Keep your unit in a plastic container with dry foliage from the area you plan to hunt. Important: Do not use wet foliage in the container because the dampness will affect the function of the camera over time. Also try carrying your unit in a Scent-Lok day pack that will remove any of the foreign odors from the unit much like it does on the human body.

- When checking the unit always carry a spare set of batteries and a memory card or roll of film in the event they are needed. The unit can be checked while baiting, but the person must be extremely scent-conscious of bait getting on the unit as mentioned earlier.

- Set the camera to a five-minute delay between pictures.

A scouting camera can be an invaluable tool to aid bear hunters, whether they are setting up their own baits or hunting with a guide. Cameras will give the hunter the critical information needed to formulate the hunt. A scouting camera will collect images of every bear at the bait so the hunter can determine the number, size, color phase, and the exact time each bear visited the bait. You can always just read the sign at a bait location, but this amounts to merely guesswork versus the accuracy of the concrete images a scouting camera provides.

Scouting cameras can also be an important tool for any guide. With them, he will have the data needed to place his hunters on the baits that are being visited by the largest animals. Scouting cameras can also be used by outfitters to get potential clients to book a hunt with their operation. They can tell the potential hunters they have scouting cameras at each bait and actually show the hunters the bears that are visiting any bait. That alone is a great selling point for any potential client and will in most cases be the deciding factor on which guide an individual selects for his bear hunt.

Keep in mind that if a hunter finds a hot spot known to produce trophy bears and the outfitter has not been using scouting cameras as an aid in his hunting or management program, there is always the option of sending a scouting camera about a month before the hunt. The guide can put it on several baits before the actual hunt to determine which bait has the greatest potential. After the hunter has invested the money and time to go on a quality bear hunt, this will determine which bait to hunt for the best opportunity for a shot at a trophy bear.

A good guide will rely on cameras to put customers on the right bait.

Some bear hunters will even send their personal cameras to the outfitter prior to the hunt as the authors did to get this image.

USING YOUR SCOUTING CAMERA FOR OTHER GAME

I think it is fair to say that scouting camera users fall into two general categories: those that use their scouting cameras primarily as functional scouting tools for deer and bear hunting, and those that use their scouting camera as an entertainment tool that extends their hunting season and enhances their hunting experience. The first group, the scouters, probably considers other game nothing more than a nuisance. In the film days, other game animals were an expensive nuisance, as they were responsible for burning up a lot of film. Squirrels, raccoons, and crows, especially, will spend excessive amounts of time at bait

9/10/06   8:26 PM   Pat Gauthier

Raccoons are usually considered a nuisance to the scouting camera enthusiast.

piles or feeders and can easily eat up a roll of film before the deer even show up. Even when using long camera delays, squirrels, raccoons, and crows were often the subject of a majority of the photos captured by a scouting camera.

Fortunately, with digital technology, the cost factor has gone away. Still, it can be frustrating to wade through dozens of small game images to get to the deer images. At least that is how the serious scouter probably feels. The same is true when scouting for bear. In fact, because bear hunting is largely done over bait, and the scouting camera is typically deployed over that bait, varmints are even more of a problem. Anyone who has sat over a bear bait knows that there can be a parade of small game visiting the bait before the bear decides to make an appearance.

The second group of scouting camera users, those interested in watching nature, are more appreciative of small game photos. They can find intrigue in a photo of raccoons interacting at a bait pile. They will get to know the various squirrels that visit a bait pile based on the squirrels' appearance. This type of scouting camera user may find himself counting the birds that appear in a single photo as opposed to cursing the fact that the birds were the subject of yet another image. This section is for the second group of hunters, in which I count myself. I can honestly say that, other than deer and bear, the only critter I have actually tried to scout was a turkey. Yet I thoroughly enjoy getting photos of all kinds of animals, large and small. Judging from the entries in the photo contests I am associated with, I am not alone. Sure, the majority of the photos submitted feature deer—and, of those, mostly bucks—but there are plenty of deer hunters who do not mind seeing a good photo of other creatures.

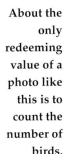

About the only redeeming value of a photo like this is to count the number of birds.

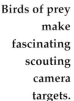

Birds of prey make fascinating scouting camera targets.

Some of these creatures, like turkeys, can be scouted and patterned like deer, and your scouting camera will provide you with information useful to your hunt. With other game, like rabbits or pheasants, for example, the photos are really just pure entertainment. Birds and animals you do not even hunt can also provide good entertainment, when it comes to your scouting camera.

Birds of prey, for example, fall into this category. Then there are the pests. These are the unknown culprits that steal your garden vegetables, dig dens under your woodpile, or put a nest under your eaves. Your scouting camera can help you identify these culprits. Finally, there are those creatures that your scouting camera catches merely by accident. Bats or songbirds are a good

8/09/06 1:05 AM

You never know what you are going to photograph; notice the bat in this photo.

example. Do not ask me why, but I have recently seen an awful lot of bats showing up in scouting camera photo contests. Perhaps it is because the motion sensors in our scouting cameras are now designed to be more sensitive and are able to sense these small animals. Here is a look at a few of the more popular species, along with a discussion on how to capture them with your scouting camera.

Scouting for Turkeys

I truly think that most scouting camera photos of turkeys are the result of the hunter wanting to participate in the hunt, beyond just sitting in the woods. The challenge of getting a great image of a big old tom turkey in strut is enough to drive a turkey hunter to deploy his cameras in the spring. Of course, the hunter can use the information provided by these photos to pattern a tom or, at least, to check out a likely hunting spot.

My scouting camera saved me some wasted turkey hunting time this past spring. I had my brother, who was hunting the weekend before I was going to hunt, affix my camera to a tree overlooking the grassy top of a ridge where I had seen birds strutting in previous years. I intended to hunt that spot during the first morning of my hunt, and I wanted to know if there was a bird using that strutting zone, and if so, just what time of day he might show up. The first thing I did when I got to the property early in the morning was to climb that ridge and check the camera. It showed absolutely no sign of a strutting tom. In fact, it showed no sign of turkeys at all. I know the camera was working because I had numerous photos of fox squirrels crossing over the top of the ridge from the big old oak trees on one side to and from the cornfield on the other. But there were no turkeys for an entire week. Needless to say, I did not hunt that area. My camera gave me some useful scouting information.

There are few more impressive images that a big tom in full strut.

Turkey hunters use scouting cameras to pattern a big tom.

Honestly, I was disappointed that I did not get a good photo of a strutting tom, backlit against the early morning sky. Then, if I were able to harvest the bird, I would have had a wonderful image to place next to my mounted fan. I guess that will have to wait until next season.

If you want a photo of a turkey, the best way is to find a strutting zone and set up your camera accordingly. Another way is to use bait. Turkeys are common visitors to bait piles of corn put out for deer and will readily come in for a free meal. You might even want to set up a turkey decoy and deploy your camera to watch the action. Eventually, a lovesick tom should show up to strut for your hen decoy. Put out a jake decoy and you might see a battle. If you are lucky, or unlucky perhaps, you might get an image of a coyote coming to eat your decoy. I have certainly seen this happen enough times while hunting. Just hope the coyote does not run off with your decoy.

Scouting for Coyotes

Besides turkeys, the animal that scouting camera users usually try to get photos of is the wily coyote. The coyote population has grown right along with the deer population, which is not surprising, given that most biologists feel that deer represent a significant part of the coyote's diet. Decades ago, when I was a youngster, coyotes were viewed primarily as a western animal. As wolf numbers plummeted, coyotes moved east. Today, coyotes thrive across the country and have become a problem on the fringe of populated areas where their existence merges with that of humans. Coyotes generally take out fawns or weaker deer, but have certainly been documented killing healthy, adult deer.

If you use your scouting cameras long enough, you will eventually get a photo of a coyote while you are scouting for deer. If you want to get a photo of a coyote, use a deer or other animal carcass for bait. Alternatively, you may use the same lure products that coyote trappers typically use to attract a coyote. A coyote den is another place to get a photo, although my experience has been that coyotes do not regularly use the same den.

I remember getting a phone call from my brother a few years ago when he had arrowed a nice buck on the outskirts of suburban Minneapolis along the Minnesota River. Unfortunately, the deer had made it to a refuge boundary and he had to wait until the next morning to retrieve it with the help of refuge authorities. Sadly, the buck did not make it very far into the refuge before expiring and, that night, the coyotes had a feast. My brother was able to salvage only a small amount of meat, as well as the buck's rack. I remember thinking how interesting it would have been to have a scouting camera set out to spy on that deer. The next time you harvest a deer, you might consider using the unused parts of the carcass for bait to try to get a good photo of some coyotes.

I have also seen a series of photos of an injured deer that coyotes dispatched. The scouting camera photos were very graphic, to say the least. As I recall, the hunter came upon the injured deer, but for legal reasons, was unable to dispatch it. So, he set up a scouting camera to see what was going to happen. The coyotes eventually found the injured deer, killed it, and ate it. Such is the way of nature.

Scouting for Wolves

Scouting for wolves is similar to scouting for coyotes. As a canine predator, a wolf would also be attracted to a deer carcass or the carcass of any other animal.

Chance photos of coyotes are more common today than ever before.

2/17/07 9:53 PM

If you want to multiply your chances of getting a coyote, put out a deer carcass.

12/28/06 2:50 AM

Wolves, like coyotes, are becoming more prolific.

12/08/06 6:30 PM

Assuming there are wolves where you scout, you might want to try deploying your scouting camera over a carcass, which should attract their attention.

Scouting for Cats

A few years ago, after taking an in-the-field lunch break from turkey hunting, I decided to change spots. While eating my sandwich, I periodically sounded my turkey call, but heard no response. As I stood and started traversing the side hill, I made eye contact with one of two tom turkeys that were silently coming in to my calls. They were just twenty-five yards away, but on the opposite side of a rise in the hillside. The first tom bolted down the hill, while his compatriot, having not seen me, scurried up over the top of the hill. I quickly set up and began making fighting purr sounds, hoping the second tom might come back. After a few minutes of calling, I sensed something and turned to look downhill to see a set of teeth coming fast. Instinctively, I rolled, and a bobcat hit right at my feet. I am not sure who was more surprised: the cat or me. As the afternoon went on, I was so flustered even a chickadee was able to startle me.

In subsequent years, I have had a lot of scouting cameras out on that property, but have yet to photograph a bobcat. Of all the local people I told the story, not one has ever seen a bobcat. However, while driving to my hunting spots early in the morning during the deer season, I have twice had bobcats cross in front of me, captured in the high beams of my truck.

I have come to the conclusion that if I want to get a photo of a bobcat, I need to put out some bait. Most of the bobcat photos submitted to scouting camera photo contests that are not the result of pure chance are captured over a carcass.

Likewise, if you want to get a photo of a mountain lion, you will need to bait it with a carcass. If you are lucky, you may come across a mountain lion kill that has been stashed for future use. This would be a wonderful place to deploy your scouting camera.

Scouting for Elk

In all my years of dealing with scouting cameras, I cannot say I have seen many good photos of elk. Scouting cameras are not big sellers out West. The majority of scouting cameras are sold to whitetail deer hunters who reside largely in the eastern half of the United States. I have brought my scouting cameras with me on elk hunts out West and set them up on trails or on a wallow, but the few photos I got are not particularly good. My biggest problem is the lack of time to get a good photo. When you hunt on public land and only for a short stint, it is not easy to get good photos. Given the time and the opportunity, I think scouting cameras would be wonderful scouting tools for elk hunters. But elk, unlike deer, tend to cover an awful lot of ground, which makes capturing them with your scouting cameras much more difficult.

Bobcats are an un-common sight, especially without something to attract them.

A carcass will attract numerous animals near the top of the food chain like this bobcat.

There are few animals more impressive than a mountain lion.

12/18/06   7:52 AM   Cuddeback

Elk can also be scouted using your scouting camera.

Scouting for Game Birds

Many deer hunters are also bird hunters. Occasionally, as a diversion, it can be fun to capture a photo of a drumming grouse, a nesting wood duck, or a colorful rooster pheasant. Good photos of drumming grouse are few and far between. It is my opinion that the proliferation of scouting cameras, which has happened only over the last few years, occurred at the same time that the ruffed grouse populations were at the bottom of their cycle. Only recently have the populations started to rebound. I fully expect, as the ruffed grouse populations grow larger, that we will see more wonderful photos of grouse on a drumming log. Pheasants also are not typically photographed. The roosters are such colorful birds that I would think more people would attempt to get a good photo of them. The populations of late have been very good and I, for one, intend to bring my scouting camera with me this fall to capture some photos of pheasants.

Waterfowl can make terrific scouting camera prey. Granted, electronics and water do not mix, but by deploying your scouting cameras along shoreline cover, you should be able to get some good photos of ducks and geese. The best time to chase waterfowl is in the spring. First of all, your scouting cameras are probably not out in the deer woods. Second, in the spring ducks' plumage is the most colorful. Perhaps the best place to get a good photo of a duck is at a wood duck nesting box. These nesting boxes are typically situated over dry land, which makes setting up your scouting camera a little more feasible.

Scouting for Small Animals

As a general rule, to get a photo of a small animal it is best either to use bait or to find its den. Every animal is a little bit different. If you want a photo of a rabbit, bait it with some vegetables. Carrots would be my first choice. Squirrels will eat corn. The shore-running animals, such as raccoons, mink, and otter, prefer

This rooster pheasant made for a colorful scouting camera subject.

Ducks are much more colorful in the spring than during the fall hunting season.

fish. Of course, anybody who uses corn to bait deer will tell you that raccoons also love corn. If you want a photo of a beaver, just find a tree that it is working on or set up your camera adjacent to its lodge. A small aspen twig can serve as bait. If you want a photo of a fox, find a fox den in spring; otherwise, trapping lure may be your best bet. Fisher can be easily attracted to your camera by stuffing fish into a hole in a log.

When trying to get a photo of a small game animal, remember to take into consideration the animal's height. Set your scouting camera accordingly. I like to put the bait on a log with my camera looking down the log. Also remember to account for the animal's size. If you locate the scouting camera the same

Make sure to account for the size of your prey when positioning your camera.

The subjects of your small game scouting are virtually limitless.

distance away from a smaller animal as you do from a deer, the animal will be very small within the photo. Your goal should be to fill as much of the frame as possible.

Scouting for Birds of Prey

If you want to get a photo of a hawk or eagle, use the carcass of a furry animal, such as a deer or rabbit, and make sure that the carcass is visible from above. Eventually, these carrion lovers will find your bait. Be sure to set up your camera low enough and close enough so the bird fills the frame.

Scouting cameras can be used to get photos of virtually any warm-blooded creature. When your camera is not in the woods scouting for deer, use it to get photos of small game animals and birds. Animals such as rabbits, squirrels, and raccoons are commonly found in backyards and make great targets, especially for the novice scouting camera user.

CHAPTER 16

Getting People Interested in the Outdoors

When I am at a hunting trade show or consumer show, many times my conversation with hunting enthusiasts leads to their favorite scouting camera photos. Every once in a while, they will even have a prized photo with them in their wallet or in a photo album, much like a photo of their kids or their latest big buck. To me, this is pretty amazing. The scouting camera world has really come of age when people carry their favorite scouting camera photos along with them to hunting shows. Quite often, the conversation then leads to another valuable attribute of scouting cameras: their ability to engage young people, wives, girlfriends, parents, grandparents, and non-hunters in the outdoors. To me, this is the frosting on the cake!

I was recently at the Minnesota State High School Boys Golf Tournament, where the team I coach was competing. I was standing on the practice green with one of my players as he stroked a few final putts before his tee time. There were probably thirty or forty high school athletes on the green at that given moment, all preparing for what was likely one of the most significant events in their young lives to date. I happened to make eye contact with one of these players, and he immediately asked me how he knew me. Caught off guard, I told him that I had been at the state tournament the previous year with one of my players who had qualified as an individual. After all, how else would a high school golfer from outstate Minnesota recognize me?

The young man, Adderly Hoag, from rural Hawley, Minnesota, announced, "No, I've seen you on the Outdoor Channel. You are on the Cuddeback commercials. You are Walt Larsen!"

I was dumbfounded. My player looked at me and exclaimed, "What?"

Adderly, as you have probably figured out, was an avid deer hunter and, like so many of us who just can't get enough, watched the Outdoor Channel, as he put it, "24/7." He told me that he owned two Cuddeback scouting cameras and that he hunted on the family farm near Hawley. Adderly and I chatted periodically during that day, whenever I came by the group he was in with one of

A scouting camera photo like this one is worthy of showing to everyone.

my players. At one point, he walked up to my father, who had come up to the tournament as an interested spectator, and announced, "I watch your son on the Outdoor Channel!"

In the days following the tournament, as I reflected on the situation, I could not help but be struck by the assertiveness shown by this young man. It is not every high school kid who, in the moments before an important event, has the wherewithal to converse with an adult that he does not know.

The experts say that it is exceedingly important that kids get involved in activities. It almost does not matter what that activity might be. Involvement is the key. Whether in sports, the arts, or the outdoors, anything that young people can use as a vehicle to grow and to become engaged is beneficial to them. Adderly was obviously involved in golf as well as in hunting, both of which, I am sure, contributed to the self-confidence that he demonstrated in conversing naturally with an adult he really did not know. I was impressed. I was also thrilled that I made a new friend, thanks to our mutual interest in scouting cameras.

Lest you think this is an isolated situation, let me share several more situations where young people, and others, were touched by the power of the scouting camera photo.

THE SCOUTING CAMERA THAT SAVED A RELATIONSHIP

A number of years ago I was in my office when I received a phone call from the single mother of a troubled boy. The mother had seen my "Candid Whitetails" column in *Deer & Deer Hunting* magazine and had called the magazine to get my phone number. She proceeded at once to scold me, thank me, and plead with me. She intimated that her son was troubled and that for the first time in his life he had shown an interest in something other than getting into trouble—an interest in a scouting camera and taking photos of deer on the family property. She went on to explain that the boy's father had left her and that, since then, she had been unable to connect with the boy. The mother had no idea where the boy had gotten the magazine, but said his request for a scouting camera was the result of my column. This boy's mother proceeded to scold me because the inexpensive scouting camera she had purchased simply did not work; worse, she had paid for the scouting camera with a credit card that she was not supposed to use. I apologized on behalf of the industry and explained that I wished she had bought a DeerCam, the film-based scouting camera I represented at the time. She then thanked me profusely for writing the column that was so engaging for her son, and started crying because she was so happy. Finally, she pleaded with me to help her get a scouting camera that worked. The last thing her son needed in his life was additional frustration. I suggested that she return the camera that she had purchased and I arranged for her to get a DeerCam at the same price.

A few weeks later, the mother called me back. She could barely talk. Once she calmed down, she told me that her son had put out his new DeerCam as soon as he received it. The next morning, before school, he announced that he was going to check it to see how many photos it had taken. She suggested it would be wise to leave the camera out for a few days, but he was out the door before she could finish her sentence. Shortly, he was back with a partially exposed roll of film that he begged her to get developed. He went off to school and she went to work, but on her lunch break she brought the film to the local Wal-Mart. She picked up the film on the way home and handed the unopened package to her son as soon as she got home. Together, they looked through a handful of photos of three different bucks. He gave his mother a hug and told her that this was the best thing that had ever happened to him.

I told the woman that I was thrilled for her, and that I hoped her son would continue to enjoy the scouting camera, and that it would also continue to bring them closer together. I also told her to encourage him to enter his photos in my "Candid Whitetails" photo contest. Honestly, I have no recollection of her name, or his name, or even where they were from. Nor do I have any idea if he ever entered one of his photos. It did not matter. I was just happy that she called me to share her story, demonstrating the power of a scouting camera photo.

A FAMILY THAT PLAYS TOGETHER, STAYS TOGETHER

When I was a teenager, my parents gave my three younger siblings and me a vote in a family decision: to join the local country club where we could swim and golf and play tennis, or to buy a cabin where we could fish, hunt, and play in the water. We chose the cabin. Many years later, my mother told me that they figured I would choose the country club, and were surprised when I sided with my younger siblings in choosing the cabin. She went on to tell me that they were even more surprised that, as we got older and went off to college, we continued to use the cabin.

Built in 1970, the cabin is still an integral part of the family, the place where many important events in our lives have occurred. My brothers both shot their first deer at the cabin, as have their kids, a number of family friends, and even their kids. For us, opening weekend of the Wisconsin gun season is a "can't miss" get-together. My first ruffed grouse and my first ring-necked pheasant were both shot at the cabin. My biggest largemouth bass came from the lake at the cabin, in spite of my regular fishing trips to places across North America.

The first scouting camera photo my brothers and I ever got was taken behind the cabin garage at a makeshift feeder. The photo was of a small doe in the fall of 1995, as I recall. That scouting camera was the first of many, and it was not just my brothers and I who participated. My sister and brother-in-law, both naturalists, took an early interest in the device from a professional standpoint. My nieces and nephews would routinely tag along as we deployed our scouting cameras or checked the film, and my mother loved to come with us on our jaunts through the woods. Naturally, everyone wanted to see what was going to be on that roll of film.

I remember one Friday night of the summer, arriving at the cabin in time for some fishing. We would keep our minnows in an old dryer drum submerged in the lake next to the dock. I was in a hurry, as I had only an hour or so of light left. The boat was ready, and all I needed was the minnows. But I soon discovered the dryer drum was empty. We would leave numerous rocks in the bottom of the drum to keep it from rolling around in the waves, and the minnows would use these rocks as cover. I moved the rocks around hopefully, but did not

This is one of the first scouting camera photos Walt ever recorded.

find a single minnow. They were all gone. So, I went off to town and bought another bunch of minnows that would easily last the weekend. You can imagine I was perturbed that my fishing time was cut in half that evening.

Still, I was not nearly as perturbed that night as I was the next morning when I discovered that all my minnows, again, were gone. I looked for holes in the drum, but there were none. I looked for raccoon tracks along the shore, but there were none. So, off to the bait shop I went again. This time, I set up my scouting camera with the hopes of catching the minnow thief. Everyone had an opinion as to the identity of the minnow thief: Was it a family of raccoons? Could it be an otter? Was it the neighborhood kingfisher? None of us were right. It turned out that the minnow thief was a great blue heron, who arose at the crack of dawn to get an expensive meal on the house. Much to the chagrin of the great blue heron, I placed a simple plywood cover on the dryer drum to save our minnows. The scouting camera had identified the thief.

Over the years at the cabin we have gotten photos of bears at the bird feeder, skunks under the porch, grouse in the yard, and fisher in the woods. Once I got up early to go fishing and discovered a bunch of fish parts on the carpeting of my new boat. My young nephews and nieces had been fishing off the boat while it was docked the previous evening. Putting two and two together, I scolded them for making a mess of my new boat. Of course, they denied doing so, and upon further review, I decided it was the work of a raccoon. The scouting camera, however, proved me wrong once again: it turned out to be an otter!

I wish I still had all of those old photos. Some of them were on the refrigerator at the cabin for a while. None of them were contest winners, but they all conjure up fond memories. They remind me of how scouting cameras have been a part of cabin lore over the past decade. Someday, my nephews and nieces will tell their kids that they grew up when scouting cameras still used film, back in the old days. Maybe they will tell how they used to check the scouting cameras with their parents, aunts, uncles, and even their grandmother. I know they will remember those good old days with fondness. Clearly, scouting cameras are one of the things that keep us going to the cabin as a family.

A TOOL FOR SCHOOL

I mentioned that my brother-in-law is a naturalist. Scott Ramsay works at the Wood Lake Nature Center in Richfield, Minnesota, a suburb of Minneapolis. It is sad to say, but one important reason that nature centers exist is to introduce city kids to a natural world they barely know. Just about every day during the school year, Wood Lake and, I presume, many other nature centers, host a field trip from a metro school. The kids are there to experience nature.

One of the biggest challenges facing a nature center is how to show the kids nature as it happens. Plants and trees and, depending on the time of year, even microorganisms and insects are all relatively available. Birds are generally available, as well. But mammals are much more difficult to present. Consider a class of third-graders walking down a nature trail. Stealthy they are not. It is certain animals can hear them coming from a long way away.

Historically, nature centers have used mounted animals inside the building as reference material. But with the advent of scouting cameras, nature centers can now also show schoolchildren photos of wild animals taken right on the premises.

My brother-in-law, Scott, uses his Cuddeback scouting camera to capture photos of the deer that make the Wood Lake Nature Center property their home. He explains to the schoolchildren the difference between bucks and does by showing them the pictures. He also explains how the bucks lose their antlers each year, and that this is the difference between antlers and horns. Scott also tells the schoolchildren that, because there is no hunting allowed in the city of Richfield, he and other nature center employees must annually reduce the deer population by trapping and dispatching some of the deer. He may even show them photos of deer at the traps, but he really uses these photos to determine the makeup of the local deer herd to determine how many deer to eliminate.

As part of the field trip, Scott gives the kids a tour of the nature center property. He shows them the fox den and then the scouting camera photos of the mother fox with her young ones. The kids even get to see a real owl nest, and then the scouting camera photos of the nest holding a mother owl and her young. Scott then shows the kids a wood duck box and photos of the drake and hen wood ducks perched atop the box, as well as a goose nest and photos of the mother goose and her goslings. He also shows a picture of a raccoon making off with some goose eggs.

Scott uses the scouting camera to challenge the kids to try to figure out what animals made different types of tracks. Based on a system that biologists historically used to determine what animals were in a given area, Scott buries a lure in the middle of a large area of moist sand. He then sets up his scouting camera to photograph the animals as they come to the lure. The children are then shown the tracks in the sand and asked what animals made the tracks. Finally, Scott uses the scouting camera photos to provide the answers.

Too many of our young people think that food comes from the grocery store. They do not have any concept of the real, natural world. Scott's scouting camera brings children nearer to a reality that, only a few generations ago, was up close and personal. The power of a photo!

NATURE IN THE BACKYARD

My mother, when she was still with us, loved to watch the wildlife in her backyard. She had feeders for every living thing, or so it seemed. She'd chase the squirrels from the bird feeders, but then hang corncobs from her crab apple tree

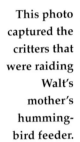

This photo captured the critters that were raiding Walt's mother's hummingbird feeder.

for them to eat. She would run the rabbits out of her garden, but then buy carrots to feed them under the pine tree.

I would frequently set up my scouting cameras to photograph my mother's backyard buddies. It gave us another fun thing to do together and to discuss. I remember her telling me about an albino squirrel. Sure enough, thanks to the scouting camera, there he was. She would talk about a gray squirrel that had no tail, too. We got a lot of photos of him. She even told me about five drake mallards that would come to eat corn. I had seen the hen mallard and two drakes, but I had a difficult time believing that there were five. The scouting camera, eventually, verified her sightings.

One day, Mom complained that something kept emptying one of her hummingbird feeders and suggested we use the scouting camera to determine the culprit. I told her that the hummingbirds were probably just extra thirsty, but she said that could not be the case. And sure enough, it turned out to be a family of raccoons that could not resist the sweet hummingbird juice. They would step up on one of her large flowerpots, trample the potted plants on their way to the feeders, and drink all the sweet nectar. You would think that, as a hunter, I would have figured it out after looking at the flowerpots. Mom just said "I told you so," and we laughed. Mothers are always right.

I GET LETTERS

As one who orchestrates the Cuddeback and other scouting camera photo contests, I get to read numerous letters or notes that accompany many of the entries. While the majority of these letters are matter-of-fact and simply describe the photo being entered, some of them go into great detail about the value of scouting cameras.

I remember one from several years ago that asked me to consider the photo being entered based on the fact that the sender's son and daughter were the ones who had selected the camera placement. The sender went on to explain that his kids went out with him to check and set his cameras, and they had shown an interest in hunting for the first time, based on their experience with the cameras. This made him pretty happy. It also made me select the photo as a finalist.

Somewhere along the way, during the film era, I got a letter from a hunter who likened the anticipation of waiting for the one-hour photo processing to the anticipation at Christmas. He said that finally getting to look at the photos was like Christmas morning and opening the long awaited gifts. I used his quote in some literature and it caught on. It also, I think, caused a lot of hunters to request scouting cameras for Christmas. What do you give to a hunter who has everything? The answer is a scouting camera, of course. Or if he already has one, a second scouting camera. Now I get countless letters from hunters who say their scouting camera is the best gift they have ever received. I also get letters about scouting cameras, given by the wife or girlfriend, ultimately resulting in the wife or girlfriend becoming involved in scouting cameras and, sometimes, even hunting. Once again, it is the power of a photo.

I have also received more than one letter chastising me for introducing the writer to something so addicting as a scouting camera. During the film era, the scouting camera addiction, like most addictions, came with a hefty and ongoing cost. The film and processing could really add up, especially if you had several scouting cameras and could not resist one-hour processing. Of course, I take those letters as disguised thank-you letters. After all, as far as I know, a scouting camera addiction never caused any serious problems.

CHAPTER 17

Wild and Crazy Ways to Use Your Scouting Camera

Scouting cameras have only recently gone mainstream. With the advent of digital photography, scouting cameras have emerged as a tool for the deer hunting masses. Because digital scouting cameras are still relatively new, how we use them is still evolving. Like the original film scouting camera, we tend to put our digital scouting cameras on trails, overlooking scrapes, and in other basic setups. But, because we no longer risk burning up expensive film, digital technology has prompted some scouting camera users to experiment more creatively.

Here are some of my favorite outside-the-box ideas that you might want to try. You will find that these ideas will add to your enjoyment in using a scouting camera.

THE GUT PILE

Quite a number of years ago, my brother Dave Larsen came up with the idea of placing our scouting camera so it overlooked the gut pile of a deer he had harvested just that morning. We were at our family cabin and he had arrowed the small buck only a few hundred yards back into the woods. He told me that he had come up with the idea after noticing how quickly gut piles from previously harvested deer would disappear. He made a mental note to try the scouting camera at the next opportunity. He wanted to see what animals took advantage of the free meal.

So we gathered the camera and made our way to the fresh gut pile. As we arrived, only a few hours after the deer had been harvested, we spooked a flock of crows. I remember thinking we were going to get twenty-four photos of crows and essentially waste the roll of film and the cost of processing.

The following weekend we walked back to where we had placed the scouting camera overlooking the gut pile and found virtually no trace of the remains and a fully exposed roll of film. Dave took the film with him and called me during the next week to tell me about the results. Yes, there were several photos

Cuddeback Digital Camera   1/16/05   6:49 AM   Non Typical' Inc

Next time you harvest a deer, put your camera on the gut pile to see what might visit.

of crows, as well as some photos of gray squirrels. That was expected. But there was also a photo of a gray fox, a critter I had personally never seen in our woods in spite of spending countless hours in my tree stand while deer hunting. There was also a photo of a red fox. More remarkable was the photo of a fisher. At that time we did not even know there were fisher in the area. We had not seen any fisher, nor had we seen any sign of them. This was pretty big news.

Since that day, we have seen plenty of fisher in our woods. They have made quite a comeback, presumably with the help of the Wisconsin DNR. But that gut pile visitor was the first. Also on that roll of film were photos of deer. It seems odd, if you look at it from a human perspective, for a deer to hang out near the remains of one of its brethren. Obviously, deer do not operate on emotion and they do not, apparently, sense any danger in this situation, either. What we found remarkable was that these deer were eating the corn that poured out from the stomach of the harvested buck. To them it was merely a pile of corn. To us, it was difficult to ignore where the corn came from.

The entire episode was very interesting and I decided to make it the subject of one of my scouting camera columns in *Deer & Deer Hunting* magazine. It seemed like perfect fodder to share with other scouting camera and deer hunting enthusiasts. The column ran with no fanfare. I received no letters, no phone calls, and no comments. However, in the months to come it was amazing how many gut pile photos I received from readers who sent them in as entries to my "Candid Whitetails" photo contest. Dave's idea started something. Today, I still see the occasional gut pile photo and, I must say, I have to smile.

11/02/06 11:11 AM

A deer carcass will attract numerous predators including birds of prey, bobcats, and coyotes.

Cuddeback Digital Camera   3/06/05 10:17 PM   Non Typical, Inc

2/05/07 9:49 PM

THE CARCASS

Somewhere along the way, hunters decided that if a gut pile made for good scouting camera bait, then a deer carcass might be even better. A carcass certainly lasts longer than a gut pile. A carcass also tends to attract an additional set of visitors. Predators like coyotes and bobcats will frequently visit a deer carcass, and so will birds of prey, such as hawks and eagles. If you decide to use a carcass to attract these birds, make sure that you make the carcass visible from the sky.

THE FENCE CROSSING

If gut piles and carcasses are not your cup of tea, there are certainly other novel scouting camera settings. One of my favorites is the fence crossing. Simply find where a trail crosses a fence and set up your camera. You can also find common fence crossing points by looking for deer hair on the barbed wire. I prefer to set my camera parallel to the fence to get a side view of deer either leaping over the fence or squeezing between the strands. Of course, you can set up the camera perpendicular to the fence as well. This setup will give you a head-on or tail-on view, both of which are interesting. Either way, you will see the athletic prowess of the whitetail deer. It really is poetry in motion.

THE WATER CROSSING

Another dramatic scouting camera setting is the water crossing. If you have a stream or creek on your property, or even a narrow point on a pond, check to see where the deer like to cross. Typically, you will find well-used trails going up and down the banks, and they will include telltale deer tracks in the mud. Unlike at

A fence crossing is perhaps the best place to get a photo that shows the true athleticism of a deer.

the fence crossing, where you can set up the camera to capture a side view, water crossings include two obstacles. First, there are typically no trees in the water on which to affix your camera. Second, you will have to contend with the angle of the banks. These banks are usually not very level. To see the deer as they cross the water, you will typically be best served by aiming your scouting camera across the water at a forty-five-degree angle, attaching the camera to the closest tree on the bank. This way, you are likely to see the deer while it is still in the water.

An alternative setup is to aim your scouting camera down the bank, to capture the deer as it hits the water from above. If you choose this tactic, be sure that your scouting camera is aimed so that it does not trigger before the deer gets to the water. Here, as with the perpendicular setup at a fence crossing, you will get both head-on and tail-on images.

THE ELEVATED SHOT

Many of the memorable moments we have as deer hunters occur while hunting from a treestand. I can personally think of numerous situations that are etched in the annals of my mind: the big Iowa buck working a scrape that I was hunting, the 8-point stud-of-a-buck in Kansas that confronted the small 6-pointer right in my shooting lane, the two forkhorns who decided to have a sparring match directly below me, the Iowa bruiser who exploded out of the cover and proceeded to chase a hot doe everywhere but within range of my stand. Each of these situations I saw from above.

Why not set your scouting camera in an elevated position, looking down on the view from a tree stand? Scrapes, community rubs, and bait piles are all conducive to an elevated setup. Sure, it takes some effort to get your camera

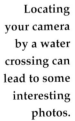

Locating your camera by a water crossing can lead to some interesting photos.

properly located, but the unique and dynamic images that you might get could certainly be worth it. It is not necessary to put the camera twenty feet up the tree. In fact, if it is that high the deer will not fill the frame. Rather, locating the camera just two to three times higher than you normally do will create the illusion of being much higher.

THE SCENTED CAMERA

So far in this book, we have both suggested that it is important that you make an effort to avoid scenting your scouting camera with either human scent or the scent of baits or lures. This rule holds especially true if you are scouting over bear bait, as bears will potentially "eat" your camera. Of course, rules are meant to be broken. You might try purposely putting scent on your camera to see what wild photos you might get. If you are going to do this with bears, by all means, make sure your camera is protected. With a deer, your biggest problem might be blurry photos caused by the deer's saliva, as it might lick your camera to taste the scent. Before you try this tactic, be sure that whatever substance you use will not attract ants and other insects that can get inside your camera and cause damage. I suggest that you place the scent or lure either on the tree behind the camera or on a stick adjacent to the camera. Better yet, put the scent on a scent pad and place the pad adjacent to the camera. This way, you minimize the chance of blurry photos.

THE MIRROR

I admit that I have never actually tried this myself, but I recall a series of photos that featured various animals and birds peering at themselves in a mirror. This scouting camera user carried a household mirror out into the woods and leaned it against a tree. Then he positioned his scouting camera at a slight angle to the mirror in order to capture over-the-shoulder shots of various forms of wildlife as they investigated the mirror. It has been quite a few years, but if memory serves, there were photos of a deer, some raccoons, and even a goose. Of all things, I would be worried that a tom turkey might see himself in the mirror and attack. The same goes for a buck during the rut. Nevertheless, I give that scouting camera user credit for thinking outside the box and coming up with a clever use for his scouting camera.

BLACK-AND-WHITE PHOTOS

If you still use a film camera, try buying some black-and-white film and using it in your scouting camera. Photography is the capturing of a three-dimensional world in two dimensions. What we see is actually the illusion of what is or was out there. By going to black-and-white, we travel further down the road of illusion and away from reality. A black-and-white image, because it lacks the color

By putting some scent near your camera, you can get some extreme close-up shots.

that defines one element in the photo from another, can be more dramatic. In essence, using black-and-white film is turning the use of your scouting camera into more of an art form.

I have no doubt there are numerous other outside-the-box ways of using a scouting camera. I hope the ones that I have suggested will trigger something in your mind. Now that we do not have to worry about wasting film, thanks to digital technology, we can try some crazy things. In the process of writing this chapter, I came up with an idea that I intend to try this fall. I want to dig a hole in a scrape large enough to hold my scouting camera so that, when the big buck comes to work the licking branch, I get a view from directly below. One of my all-time favorite photographs, not a scouting camera photo, was a shot of my brother sitting in a treestand. The photographer was below the treestand looking directly up into the sky through the slats in the treestand. It was a dramatic view and one that I hope to duplicate with a deer and my scouting camera. I hope, though, a big buck does not decide to tear up the scrape and, in the process, my scouting camera. Stay tuned.

CHAPTER 18

Taking Award-Winning Photos with Your Scouting Camera

SCOUTING CAMERA PHOTO CONTEST HISTORY

In the mid-1990s, I received a call from an ad sales representative at *Deer & Deer Hunting* magazine. She told me of a small company in Georgia that made a device designed to take photos of deer. She explained further that this company was considering throwing in the proverbial towel, as sales for their products had not been what they had hoped for. She apparently told them that I could help.

That is how I first got involved in the world of scouting cameras. That company was CamTrakker, and I was soon putting together a mailing on their behalf, to be sent to their rather modest mailing list. The mailer, it turned out, worked remarkably well. Roughly 25 percent of the people who received it plunked down $429, plus a healthy shipping and handling charge, to try out this remote scouting camera. I found the premise of the scouting camera to be very compelling and, apparently, so did a lot of others.

Sometime between that hunting season and the next, I was asked to be the judge in a photo contest for patrons of the Hennepin County Park system in suburban Minneapolis. My sister, Dana Larsen-Ramsay, was employed by the Park and suggested that I might be a good judge. Truth be told, I knew little about photography, but I still found the opportunity intriguing. As I was judging, I could not help but notice the tremendous passion that these amateur photographers were showing for the photos, and not just for their own photos. Each of them spent considerable time behind the ropes discussing and admiring each and every photo. I found this quite interesting and made a mental note.

In the next several months, I had a brainstorm. Actually, I just connected the dots. "Why not have scouting camera photo contests?" I surmised. The selection of scouting camera photos I had to choose from in assembling the mailing for CamTrakker was minimal. There were only a few nice photos. In the end, I decided the scouting camera photos would sell the scouting cameras. A photo contest would compel scouting camera users to submit their favorite photos, which I would then be able to use for marketing purposes. Contest participants could win prizes and would see their photos in a brochure of finalists. If the scouting camera users exhibited anywhere near the passion I had seen in the Park contest photographers, my plan would work. In fact, the plan worked beyond my wildest dreams. As the orchestrator of the CamTrakker photo contest, I received quite a few photos the first year and the volume grew exponentially as the photos were used to advertise the product.

In time, Pat Durkin, the editor of *Deer & Deer Hunting* magazine at the time, called to suggest, since I had a few years' worth of photos, that I write a column featuring the photos for the magazine. That conversation spawned my column, "Candid Whitetails." Eventually, it also spawned a "Candid Whitetails" photo contest.

The CamTrakker photo contest was one that I personally judged. I would select the finalists in each of several categories and then have family and friends vote for their favorites. I used large, rectangular sheets of foam core that had two strips of Velcro running horizontally from one end to the other. Each individual photo was mounted to a four-by-six-inch piece of foam core that had the opposite Velcro attached to its back. I would spend hours shuffling and reshuffling the photos within their respective categories until I had the winning order. Then, I would select from among the top photos in each category and arrive at a top twenty overall.

We created a web site for the "Candid Whitetails" contest where the readers of *Deer & Deer Hunting* could vote for their favorite photo among eight finalists in each of six categories. I select the eight finalists and the readers picked the winner.

After my early association with CamTrakker, I hooked up with Non Typical, Inc., the makers of DeerCam. I again initiated a photo contest in which I judged the entries. The DeerCam photo contest was quite streamlined and offered DeerCams as prizes for each of three categories. I used the photos as advertising ammunition, although DeerCam was certainly established by the time I got involved. With the digital age upon us, Mark Cuddeback, owner of NonTypical, developed the Cuddeback digital scouting camera, and with the new brand, came a new photo contest. The Cuddeback photo contest is the king of all scouting camera photo contests. Thousands of images are entered in the contest each year. Plus, there is a separate contest for Cuddeback video clips. Both Cuddeback contests feature images taken by Cuddeback scouting cameras. I select the finalists and visitors to the Cuddeback web site vote for the winners. But we have added a new twist: the finalists are now placed in a tournament bracket so that visitors to the Cuddeback web site can vote for a winner in each head-to-head pairing. It works just like an NCAA college basketball tournament bracket, but consumers like you determine the outcome. Each round takes a month and, with sixty-four finalists, the contest takes six months. People enjoy it because they get to vote six times through the course of the event.

HOW TO GET A CONTEST-WORTHY SCOUTING CAMERA PHOTO

I have been the orchestrator of four different scouting camera photo contests over a period of more than a decade. In two of these contests, I selected the winners. In the other two contests I select the finalists, and the public chooses the winners. From all of this experience, this is what I have gleaned. Here are my suggestions as to how you can capture an award-winning photo:

- **You Cannot Beat an Impressive Rack**

  If you want to win a scouting camera photo contest, your best bet is to enter an image of a big buck with a very large set of antlers. This is not exactly an earth-shattering revelation, I know. But, the fact is, the vast majority of all photo contest winners are monster bucks. Let's face it: the ultimate goal of most deer hunters is a trophy for the wall. Should it be any different in a photo contest for deer hunters? So how do you get a photo of a big buck? You need to put your scouting camera where there are many bucks, and your odds are multiplied if you use multiple cameras. Most of the winners come from the states of Kansas, Iowa, Illinois, and Wisconsin because these states are where most of the big bucks live.

Nothing beats a big set of antlers when it comes to a photo contest.

Cuddeback Digital Camera 11/03/05 9:54 AM Non Typical, Inc

Photos taken during the day have a higher preference by photo contest voters than nighttime photos.

A big buck that fills the frame will fare well in a photo contest.

- **A Good Daytime Image Trumps a Good Nighttime Image**
  More often than not, an image captured during the day will beat one captured at night. This is the case for three reasons. First, a daytime photo, especially of a big buck, is more difficult to get than a nighttime photo. Second, a daytime photo better represents what we, as hunters, aspire to—a big buck in our sights during shooting hours. Third, daytime photos are more colorful, and therefore more appealing, than nighttime photos.

- **A Close-up Shot Beats a Distant Shot**
  That a close-up shot would be preferred to a distant shot might be another obvious observation but the majority of images submitted to contests

This may be a really big buck, but is just too far away from the camera.

feature deer that are too far away from the camera. People simply set their cameras too far away from their intended quarry. Ten feet is plenty far away. Twenty feet is too far away. The reason people set their cameras too far away is that they are afraid the deer will get past the camera before it triggers. The solution to this is either to buy a faster-triggering camera or to set the camera so that the deer is quartering to or from it. In this way, the deer is in the capture zone for a longer period of time.

- **An Engaged Big Buck Beats a Non-Engaged Big Buck**
  What do I mean by engaged? This is difficult to explain, and yet almost universal. If the big buck in your photo looks like he is involved or engaged in an activity, that photo will fare better than if he is not. For example, if he is pawing a scrape, working a licking branch, nosing a rub, striking a regal pose, or sniffing the ground, and you can still easily see his rack, you have got a potential winning photo. Voters look for reasons to choose one big buck photo over another, and an element of interest will separate the winner from the loser. Obviously, you cannot determine when your camera takes the photo, so you cannot fully control the composition of the photo. However, to stack the odds in your favor, place your camera where the big buck, should he get his photo taken, would be engaged.
  Interestingly, photos of big bucks in fast action do not fare nearly as well as photos of big bucks that are more involved. Photos of two big bucks fighting, or of a big buck taking on a decoy, always do well, but almost never win. These action shots always seem to lose out to an excellent photo of an involved big buck. My theory is that while an action shot is interesting, it is not what we commonly see while we are hunting. Excessive action also makes it more difficult to see the size of the antlers.

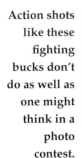

A buck working a licking branch is a photo contest voter favorite.

Cuddeback Digital Camera 10/11/05 2:33 AM   Non Typical, Inc

Action shots like these fighting bucks don't do as well as one might think in a photo contest.

1/10/07 5:59 PM   Cuddeback

- **Natural Photos Are Superior to Unnatural Photos**
  If you want to win a scouting camera photo contest, then skip the feeder, the bait, and the scent dripper. Hunters want to see a scouting camera photo that resembles what they want to see in the wild, and that is a deer acting naturally in its unadulterated, natural surroundings.

- **Rut-Time Photos Beat Photos from Any Other Season**
  Once again, we hunters want to see in a scouting camera photo just what we want to see while in a stand: a big buck during the rut. Photos of big bucks in velvet are nice, but they do not win a photo contest. Even photos of hard-antlered deer taken early in the season in the colorful October

If at all possible, avoid inclusion of unnatural objects in your photo.

10/07/06 2:03 AM

Photo contest voters like a rutting big buck with a big neck and the look of an NFL linebacker.

10/26/05 6:47 PM   Young

A quartering view of a big buck helps us see all the tines on his rack.

10/24/06 6:59 PM   John Georgen

woods will not beat the big buck with his swollen neck in the relatively colorless November woods.

- **A Quartering View of the Rack Beats a Profile or Head-On**
  This one is easy to explain. The more of a big rack we see, the better your photo will fare. Try to set up your shot so the buck is likely to give you a quartering view of his antlers. You might even want to direct him with some carefully placed, natural-looking barriers.

- **A Clean, Simple Foreground and Background Beat the Opposite**
  The one thing that ruins an otherwise outstanding big buck photo is the failure to remove a branch or brush between your camera and the deer. This is a shame because it is so easy to fix. Remove all such obstacles, as they are a distraction during daylight hours and, worse, they will reflect the flash at night. Likewise, look at your background. A mass of limbs or branches roughly the size of antler tines will cause antlers to disappear. Sometimes, night photos will fare better than day photos simply because the background, thanks to the darkness, is clean. Snow can also make a wonderful background, as it provides great contrast to the deer and his antlers.

- **Midwestern Bucks Beat Bucks from Other Regions**
  Large-bodied deer, with racks that have both good mass and tine length, almost always win scouting camera photo contests. This describes the bucks from Kansas, Iowa, Illinois, Wisconsin, and neighboring states.

A busy foreground or background can distract from our view of the deer's antlers.

1/09/07 12:01 AM   Harry Benson

Snow makes for wonderful body and antler contrast.

11/30/06 2:43 PM

Contest voters prefer midwestern bucks like this guy from Wisconsin.

10/31/05 4:42 AM   Kenneuberger

A rack that is too non-typical does not fare as well as one might think in a photo contest.

1/12/07 4:33 PM

A buck with a 10- or 12- point rack appeals to the voters.

These are also the deer you see gracing the covers of various magazines. Why? Big bucks sell more magazines.

- **Typical Beats Non-Typical**
  People are more apt to "ooh and aah" over an extremely non-typical rack, but when it comes to picking their favorite scouting camera photo, a typical rack will win just about every time.

- **10- or 12-Pointers are Preferred**
  The best way to explain this observation is to ask any deer hunter what he would prefer on his wall. More often than not he will choose a classic 10- or 12-point buck rather than anything else. In a scouting camera photo, a buck that has enough tines to fill the space in the photo looks better than one that does not. At the same time, a buck with too much going on in its antlers makes it difficult, in a two-dimensional photo, to really see the rack.

- **Tine Length Beats Width; Width Beats Mass**
  Not that you can choose the dynamics of the antlers on the buck you photograph, but voters seem to prefer tine length first, width second, and mass third. My opinion is that tine length tends to fill up space in a two-dimensional photo better than width or mass and, therefore, makes for a more impressive photo. I am not so sure that voters would have the same feelings if the racks were lying on a table in front of them.

Tine length, as this buck has, is preferred over antler width or mass.

Drop tines and sticker points add an element of character.

- **Drop Tines and Sticker Points are a Good Thing**
  Wait a minute: drop tines and sticker points are non-typical points, right? Well, yes, they are, but scouting camera photo contest voters like both drop tines and sticker points—but in moderation. Extremely non-typical points do not cut it. Simple, clean, distinctive drop tines and sticker points add a little character and a few more votes.

The drama and color of a sunrise or sunset can help your photo stand out.

Elevating your camera can create added interest to your photo.

- **Images Taken at Dawn or Dusk Are a Plus**

  It can be risky to aim your scouting camera in the direction of the rising or setting sun, but doing so gives you the opportunity to capture your subject, the big buck, with a dramatic sunrise or sunset in the background. Of course, aiming your camera at the sun also introduces the chance of the big buck appearing so backlit that you cannot see any detail. Still, the color from the sunrise or sunset gives you that extra edge that will entice the voters to choose your photo over another.

OTHER TECHNIQUES FOR CAPTURING INTERESTING IMAGES

There are other photographic techniques that can be applied to scouting cameras that will help you to get better photos. While these are not necessarily techniques that have proven advantageous in a photo contest, they will make for more interesting and compositionally engaging images.

Unusual Point of View

Virtually every scouting camera user affixes his camera roughly thirty inches off the ground, aiming to get a straight-on image of passing deer. The result is that all images look pretty much the same. Try locating your camera slightly lower and aiming it so as to be looking up at your subject. This perspective will make a big buck look even more majestic and can also bring more sky into play as a background. Likewise, setting your camera somewhat higher than usual will give you the unique perspective of looking down into the deer's rack. This perspective is consistent with how we see many deer while hunting from above in a treestand.

Set Up for an Interesting Background

One of my favorite early scouting camera photos was of a small buck I captured in suburban Minneapolis, not far from my home. I positioned the camera so that the local water tower would appear in the background, thereby identifying the deer as a suburban resident. Although contest voters may prefer a natural background, of all the photos I have in my album, this one got a lot of attention because of its unique background. You might try to use the family farm, your house or cabin, an office building, an old tractor, your treestand, or some other unexpected item in the background of your photos.

Frame Your Subject

A secret technique that professional photographers use is to frame their subject with a doorway, a window, an archway, or foliage. Framing the subject places greater emphasis on it. This is why we frame paintings. You, too, can use this technique, although you will have to be very careful that your frame does not cause flashback. Positioning your camera to frame the deer inside colorful leaves or between cornrows can add a dramatic effect to your photo.

The Rule of Thirds

The photographer's rule of thirds states that if you divide your frame vertically and horizontally in thirds, and position your subject at the intersection of any of these lines, it will have additional impact. To take advantage of this rule, position your camera so that the deer will likely have its head at one of these intersections. If you have a stump in your background, for example, locate it at one of these intersections. Or if you have a predominant tree in your frame, do not center it. Instead, have it running along either the left or right third of the photo.

The local water tower in the background of this photo made it a favorite.

The family farm in the background of this photo adds color and story appeal.

11/04/06 7:09 AM   Buckmaster   Cuddeback

The feeder in this photo serves to frame the subjects.

7/19/06 8:51 AM   Cuddeback

The brushline in this photo spans the bottom third of the image, which is consistent with the photographer's rule of thirds.

4/11/07 3:54 PM   Todd Reabe   CB1   Cuddeback

This tom turkey was captured at the intersection of the bottom and right-hand thirds of the frame.

4/26/07 1:28 PM   Todd Reabe   CB1   Cuddeback

This photo combines an interesting background (cabin) and foreground element (turkey target), which attracted the real turkeys.

4/15/07 6:16 PM   Autumn's Acres   Cuddeback

The water in the fore-ground of this photo provides an element of interest.

9/28/06 6:03 PM

Likewise, any horizontal line—be it the horizon, a downed tree, or the top of the standing cornfield—should run either along the top or bottom third of the frame.

Elements of Interest in the Foreground

Another trick professional photographers use is to guide your eye to the subject via an element in the foreground. They will commonly use railings or roads or fences to direct us to the primary subject. You can also employ this technique by aiming the camera down a licking branch, for example, which will lead the eye to the deer working the licking branch. The professional photographer may shoot a building with a flowerpot in the foreground, while you may use a color-ful leaf hanging from a branch in your foreground. Once again, your flash will overexpose anything too close to the camera, so be careful.

I am constantly amazed at the lack of creativity when it comes to scouting camera photos. Granted, scouting cameras are tools to find deer and not tools of art. Still, I would rather have an aesthetically pleasing photo of a big buck than a lousy photo of a big buck. By paying attention to some simple rules gleaned from photo contests and borrowing tricks from professional photographers, you can capture some interesting, award-winning scouting camera photos.

CHAPTER 19

Using Your Scouting Camera as a General Surveillance Tool

Scouting cameras are, in essence, surveillance devices designed to monitor the activities of deer, bear, and other game. The fact is, while scouting cameras are designed specifically for this particular use, they can also make excellent, inexpensive, easy-to-use general surveillance devices as well. Anything that gives off heat and is in motion will trigger your scouting camera. This means the surveillance possibilities are truly endless. Use your imagination and you will discover a myriad of possibilities.

The only real disadvantage of a scouting camera that is designed for use as a hunting tool being used as a general surveillance device is the flash. Obviously, this is a significant disadvantage if you are trying to monitor people at night who would prefer not to be monitored. Even the latest "no flash" infrared technology that does not spook game can be seen by humans. Although discreet, the infrared system appears red to the human eye when activated. Still, given that general surveillance use is a bonus above and beyond the intended use of the product, this limitation should not preclude you from getting additional use out of your scouting camera.

Perhaps the best way to demonstrate the breadth of general surveillance uses for your scouting camera is to offer examples that I have heard about over my years of dealing with scouting cameras. Some of them are obvious and expected, while others are really quite clever. Together, they should give you an idea of how others have used their scouting cameras as general surveillance tools. I will leave it up to you to translate these into ideas and uses of your own.

MONITORING TRESPASSERS
The most common general surveillance use of a scouting camera, that does not involve hunting, is scouting for trespassers. Sometimes this is intended, and sometimes it happens accidentally when a scouting camera is being used for game. A hunter sets up his scouting camera hoping to get an image of a big buck and instead gets a photo of his neighbor, his hunting buddy, the local

If you are worried about vandalism, let your scouting camera catch the vandal red-handed.

Your scouting camera can also help you to catch trespassers.

poacher, or the neighbor's dog. Stories of this nature are plentiful and have, no doubt, resulted in some not-so-pleasant confrontations. When a hunter is hunting on private land and finds out he has unauthorized competition, he is generally not very happy.

Of course, sometimes the hunter suspects trespassing and, therefore, sets up his scouting camera with the express intent of catching the bad guy. Scouting cameras are ideal for this, so long as the bad guy does not see the camera. Fortunately, most scouting cameras have the ability to be set for daytime-only operation. This feature eliminates the flash problem. It does not, however, eliminate the possibility of the trespasser spotting the scouting camera. Theft of scouting cameras is a problem, and I suspect a good portion of the theft occurs when somebody is afraid that his photo has been taken, and theft is the only way to eliminate the evidence. Here are a few of my favorite trespassing stories.

The New Neighbor
A fellow hunter told me about his new hunting property and how he was really enjoying the process of managing the land for deer hunting. He had planted several food plots and was generally refurbishing the acreage for the benefit of the deer. He purchased several scouting cameras with the intention of watching the fruits of his labor. Over time, the property began to produce, and he enjoyed seeing photos of the resident deer. His neighbor, who had apparently always had permission to hunt the land from the previous landowner, was not so thrilled. He apparently felt entitled to continue hunting there, and helped himself in spite of the no trespassing signs and an earlier conversation. What he did not expect was for the scouting camera to take his photo. He noticed the camera and, fearing capture, swiped it. What he did not realize, though, was that as he was leaving the scene of the crime, yet another scouting camera caught him in the act, the stolen scouting camera in hand.

When the sheriff arrived to confront the neighbor, he denied the accusation. When the sheriff showed him the photo, he eventually admitted to trespassing. When the sheriff asked where the stolen camera was, the neighbor eventually explained: it had occurred to him as he was leaving the property that other cameras might be in use, so he tossed the stolen camera into a nearby pond. The sheriff took this as an admission that he did not intend to steal the camera to destroy the camera itself, but to destroy the evidence of his trespassing. "It's still theft," the sheriff reminded him.

The Unlikely Building Materials Thief
A couple of hunting buddies had saved their money to buy hunting land and were in the process of building a modest hunting cabin on their new property. Each weekend, they would hunt in the morning, work through midday, and hunt again in the evening. The cabin site was remote enough, they thought, that leaving some building materials unattended during the week would not be a problem. As their first season went along, they began to notice small amounts of materials missing. At first, they each figured the other was using the materials in the building process. Eventually, they realized that both parties were wondering the same thing: where were the materials going? So, they pulled one of their scouting cameras from its spot in the woods and set it up on the building site. They set it for day-only and could not wait until the next weekend to see what the scouting camera found.

The two hunters were astonished to find that an elderly woman, a neighbor they had not met, was the thief. She did not drive to the site, so as to avoid suspicion, but would take small amounts of building materials each week because she was physically unable to carry much more. Why did she steal the materials? When the hunters ultimately confronted her by showing her the photo, she was obviously ashamed and visibly embarrassed. The hunters, after a discussion between themselves, opted not to report her to the authorities, but they did ask her why she was taking the materials. She told them that she could not afford to purchase such materials and was using them to prepare her rundown house for the impending winter. The hunters asked her to please stop stealing their materials and then offered to help her with her house. She, in turn, promised not to take any more building materials, and kept her promise.

The Treestand Kidnapper

Here is another example of a hunter who had a crazy experience. Each weekend, the hunter would head to his hunting shack for a quiet weekend of bowhunting. He had several stands set up on his property, but since he had seen a magnificent buck on opening weekend from one particular stand along a cornfield, he tended to hunt that stand the most. Several weekends into the season, while on stand, he consciously noticed what he had subconsciously noted before: that his treestand seemed to be set at a slightly different angle. Perplexed, he turned toward the tree and looked at the trunk for signs of where he had originally affixed the stand. Sure enough, the tree stand had been moved. But how? And why? After pondering the situation, he decided to let his scouting camera be the sleuth.

The hunter set the scouting camera near the ground adjacent to the tree and did his best to camouflage it. The next weekend, he had his answer. At least, he had part of it. A young man made off with his stand on Monday and then returned it on Friday. Knowing the hunter hunted only on weekends, the young man, he discovered, was borrowing the stand for his own use. He was always careful to bring it back and set it up again before the weekend. Showing the photo around town without explanation, the hunter soon discovered the identity of the young man and called him on the phone. It seems the young man could not afford his own treestand, and he, too, had seen the big buck, but on his side of the fence. The hunter felt that the young man should know better, and that to make restitution he should do some chores on the hunter's property. In the end, satisfied that the young man had learned his lesson, the hunter gave the young man an old treestand that he no longer used. Ultimately, the two became hunting buddies.

Not all scouting camera surveillance use involves hunting or hunting land. Here are some non-hunting examples of people using their scouting camera as a surveillance tool.

How to Select an Honest Contractor

A logging company in the Pacific Northwest would deposit trees in a central location and sell the logs by the truckload to independent contractors. These contractors would self-report the number of loads they took, and they would be billed accordingly. Never did the math quite work out. Somebody always seemed to be fudging the number of truckloads. But because there were several independent contractors, the logging company had no way to figure out who was being dishonest. One day, a logging company employee, who happened to own a scouting camera, suggested a scouting camera would solve the problem. Since logging trucks give off heat, a scouting camera would take their photo. In time, the logging company was able to determine which contractors were honest and which ones were not. This was a simple, clever way to solve a problem by using a scouting camera as a surveillance device.

THE CURFEW COP

I am not sure what the parenting experts would say about this next scenario, but it does demonstrate another way to use scouting cameras as surveillance tools. A single mother, tired of confrontations with her teenage son regarding curfew violations, decided to borrow a neighbor's scouting camera to monitor exactly when her son returned home. She theorized that if she went to bed instead of waiting up for her son, it would show trust and eliminate the uncomfortable conversation when he walked in the door. She set the camera in the woods along the driveway, well away from the house, so as to be as discreet as possible. The camera would capture an image of the vehicle as it drove by. In the morning, on her daily walk, she would check the camera while he was still sleeping. After several weekends, she was confident that he did indeed follow the curfew rules she had set, and she returned the camera to her neighbor. Her son was unaware of her surveillance tactics and their relationship was less strained.

CAPTURE THE KIDS WITH YOUR SCOUTING CAMERAS

An enterprising father, tired of a household of kids playing video games, decided to bring the video game to life. He took his scouting cameras and showed the youngsters how to use them. Behind his house was a small woodlot with a series of trails. The premise of the game was to set the cameras on the trails and let the kids go from one end of the woodlot to the other without leaving a trail and without ever turning back. The cameras were set up so that there was always a way to make it through without getting photographed. The kids loved the game and soon created their own variations, including using the cameras as checkpoints in a corn maze. In that game, the first person through the maze, with their photo taken by each camera, was the winner. Sure, the kids still played video games, but far less often than before they were introduced to the scouting camera game.

Kids will have fun getting captured by the camera.

As you can imagine, there are numerous police departments, private investigators, and the like that have used scouting cameras designed for hunters to capture images of people doing things they are not supposed to do. Visual evidence is a powerful tool, not only in court, but also when presented directly to the perpetrator.

USING THE TIME-LAPSE MODE ON YOUR SCOUTING CAMERA

Some of the better digital scouting cameras have a time-lapse feature, whereby you set the camera to automatically capture an image at given intervals of time. The camera is automatically triggered as programmed. In this mode, an animal walking by will not trigger the camera. The time-lapse feature allows you to monitor progress or change and, in its own way, is another form of surveillance.

Here are a few common uses for the time-lapse mode:

Monitoring the Growth of Your Food Plot

Food plots are an important part of the modern deer hunter's repertoire. Since most hunters do not get to watch their food plot grow, it is interesting to see the progress captured on a daily basis by a scouting camera in time-lapse mode. Even if you live where you can see your food plot grow, having a record of the growth allows you to show others. You will notice spurts of growth after a good rain and a lack of growth during a drought. You will also see when the deer and other critters first discover your food plot, especially if you set your camera to take images either earlier or later in the day.

Watching Your Garden Grow

The time-lapse mode in your scouting camera is also ideal for watching your garden grow. A garden can be even more interesting to watch than a food plot because of the variety of plants. You will be able to see which vegetables come up and when. Over the years, if you do it annually, you will be able to compare the dates when the tomatoes ripen or the pumpkins first appear. A flower garden may be even better, as the time-lapse mode will capture it in all of its various states of splendor. Not only will the images be beautiful, but they will also give you a record of what flowers bloom and when. Again, comparing over the years can be interesting, especially for the garden fanatic.

Theater of the Seasons

You have probably seen this done before by videographers: they meld together 365 days worth of footage looking at the same scene. You can do the same thing with your scouting camera set up in time-lapse mode. A lake scene would be a good subject. In the spring, there is a burst of life as the area surrounding the lake begins to green up. By summer, the water is blue and the shoreline is vivid green. Autumn goes the other direction, as the color transitions from vivid yellow, orange, and red into bleak browns and grays. With winter, the water freezes and the snow blankets the landscape. With your scouting camera in time-lapse mode, you can create your own theater of the seasons using your favorite vista.

Monitoring a Building Project

Another common use of the time-lapse mode on your scouting camera is to monitor a building project. Such monitoring is both interesting and informational. Should you have a disagreement with the builder, the time-lapse mode photos can serve as evidence. Beyond that, watching a building go up offers similar enjoyment to watching your food plot or garden grow. There is a sense of satisfaction as you see the progress. It is especially impressive to watch the early stages, as the building is framed and quickly starts to take shape.

Scouting cameras are really just surveillance devices designed for deer hunters. When your scouting cameras are not in the woods, consider using them to monitor other events. The possible uses are limited only by your imagination.

TIME-LAPSE PHOTOS SHOW THE PROGRESS
OF A BUILDING PROJECT

6/19/06   3:00 PM   Mark Cuddeback

6/19/06   7:00 PM   Mark Cuddeback

TIME-LAPSE PHOTOS SHOW THE PROGRESS
OF A BUILDING PROJECT

CHAPTER 20

The Changing Technology in Scouting Cameras

It was the late 1990s and I had drawn a coveted Iowa bow tag. My first trip down was futile, as daytime temperatures approached eighty degrees Fahrenheit. After a couple days of poor hunting, and seeing that the forecast called for more unseasonably warm weather, I decided to leave early and save my vacation days for when hunting would be better. The one positive thing about that first trip was that the locals told me of a big buck that they had frequently watched on our property. So before departing, I deployed my scouting cameras with the hope of capturing an image or two of the monster. I wanted visual proof before I got too excited, as everyone's definition of "big" is different.

The next time I went down brought much more favorable weather. It was cold and approaching that time of the season when the early part of the rut might very well kick in. The first thing I did, of course, was to change out the rolls of film from my scouting cameras and hightail it into town and the one-hour film processor. It was midday, so I was not too concerned about missing good hunting time. When I got the film back, I quickly rifled through the prints, only to find that the bulk of the photos were of squirrels. The few deer that appeared were all small. I was frustrated, first of all, that I had used rolls of 24-exposure film instead of 36-exposure film. I was even more frustrated when I looked at the time stamp on the photos: all twenty-four photos had been taken in the first two days—those hot days I had opted not to hunt.

As I sat on stand that night, trying to stay warm, as the temperatures were now in the twenties, I could not help but notice flock after flock of northern mallards pouring into a wide spot in a creek several hundred yards away. The same thing happened the next morning. I could not resist the temptation, and went to town at lunchtime to buy a duck stamp and whatever else I needed to hunt ducks.

Even with my duck stamp in hand, I decided to return to my stand. That evening produced no big deer. Nor did the next morning. Tired of freezing, and having not seen the big buck, while at the same time being tempted by a growing flock of big northern greenheads, I opted for the shotgun that afternoon. The hunt was memorable. The ducks just kept coming, and I easily bagged a limit of nice drakes, one of which adorns my office wall today. Realizing that I still had time to get on stand yet that evening, I hurried back to my truck to change clothes. As I was frantically trying to get ready, I looked up the coulee where I had my stand, only to see the big buck. He proceeded to walk right past my stand. I almost threw up I was so upset. I still think of that sinking feeling every time I look at the mounted drake mallard in my office. It was a once-in-a-lifetime buck. Even at several hundred yards, I could easily see he carried a magnificent rack.

One of the locals happened to drive by a few minutes later and informed me that he had seen the big buck cross the coulee several times since I had been down last, typically about that time of the evening. I thanked him for the information and hustled to my stand with the fleeting hope that the buck just might come back. In spite of spending a lot of the season's afternoons in that stand, I never did see him. Interestingly, I never got his photo either.

What bothered me more than anything was knowing that the buck had probably walked past my cameras several times between my two hunts, but not until the film had been used up. Had I seen him on film, I know I would have stayed on stand, forgoing any mallard hunt. Of course, this does not mean I would have bagged this big buck, but I certainly would have gotten the opportunity to see him up close. In essence, film technology cost me a shot at that buck.

I dare say that nobody was more enamored with the premise of scouting cameras in the film days than I was, in spite of the film and processing costs, and the limitations imposed by a roll of film. Other enthusiasts also tolerated the disadvantages of film, and some racked up some pretty hefty processing bills.

So when digital technology hit the consumer market and, in turn, the scouting camera market, those of us who had been addicted to the film version of the product rejoiced. What we did not realize was how hamstrung we had been by the film cameras. It was nothing to get a hundred images on our digital scouting cameras during the same amount of time we used to get just twenty-four prints from our film cameras. I remember getting quite a few letters from photo contest participants who claimed to get several hundred images in a very short time. Thank goodness for digital.

Digital camera technology revolutionized scouting cameras and was responsible for bringing scouting cameras to the mainstream. Sure, we had to relearn how to use our scouting cameras, given the new technology, but this was a small price to pay when we were no longer limited to twenty-four or thirty-six photos or required to visit a film processor.

This nice Iowa buck happened to be the thirty-eighth image on my memory card. Had I been using a film camera, I would have never captured him.

Such watershed revolutions are not everyday occurrences. In the hunting industry, I have been fortunate enough to be connected to a few such revolutions over the years, including single cam bows, carbon clothes, and layered archery targets, besides digital scouting cameras. None of these categories has been truly revolutionized again, at least not so far. Yet, products in each of these categories continue to evolve, getting better and better.

So what is the future for scouting cameras? Here are my thoughts:

WILL SCOUTING CAMERAS SHRINK?

If you want to know what is coming next in the world of digital scouting cameras, watch what happens in the consumer digital camera market. In the past few years, the big change has been the incredible shrinking camera. Smaller cameras make sense, given that people like to carry their digital camera with them wherever they go. The scouting camera manufacturers have not taken up this phenomenon because it is not necessary. Hunters do not carry their scouting cameras with them all day long. So there is no need for a pocket-sized scouting camera. If anything, a diminutive scouting camera might be a disadvantage, as it would be more difficult to find. I don't know about you, but I have had to look hard for my relatively large scouting cameras on more than one occasion.

IS VIDEO THE NEXT FRONTIER?

Some think video scouting cameras may replace the existing still image scouting cameras. I do not agree. In the consumer market, sales of digital still cameras continue to be very strong, especially given the size innovation. Sales of video cameras, on the other hand, have peaked and fallen off. In the 1990s, it seemed everyone had and used a video camera. Even as these cameras went digital, became smaller and less expensive, they also seemed to spend more time in the closet.

In the scouting camera market, straight video cameras have really gone nowhere. Granted, they are bulky and expensive, but if they really were the future I think they would at least have gained a small cult following. I just do not see that. Besides, my Cuddeback takes video clips already. I can set it up to record video clips from ten seconds to one minute long. I even get an accompanying still image with each video clip taken. Video clips are fun, but judging from the photo contest entries that I see, only a small percentage of the scouting camera owners use video clips. I also have the ability to take video clips with my cell phone. Do I use it? Rarely. Will this change? Watch the consumer market. If video becomes a big deal with changing technology, that is where it will first flourish.

WILL SCOUTING CAMERAS TURN INTO WEB CAMS?

There are places on the Internet where you can watch a particular hunting spot all day long, every day of the year. Is this web cam technology the next scouting camera frontier? I ask you, have you ever watched these web sites? In my opinion, they make watching paint dry or grass grow seem exciting. You know what it is like to be on stand for hours on end without any activity. At least on stand you know it is part of the hunting game. But can you imagine doing it from home? I cannot.

WILL MY SCOUTING CAMERA EMAIL IMAGES VIA CELL PHONE?

What if your scouting camera was able to email you each image it took via a cell phone connection? Well, this technology exists and has been on the market. You, the consumer, have decided, so far, that it is not worth the price. Here is how it works: the photo is taken and compressed as necessary. The camera then sends the image, via cell phone, to a central hub. The hub identifies the camera and the owner and, in turn, emails it to your email account. You get the image only minutes after it was taken. It is really rather compelling. Why, then, has it not taken off? First of all, as you know if you have tried to use your cell phone in rural America, cell phone service is not exceptionally reliable, at least not yet. Is it reliable enough? In many places, yes, it is. Second, the cost for one of these units is relatively significant, although not outrageous. Third, and this is the killer, you must pay a monthly fee for this service. Just like with your cable TV or your cell phone contract, you will be charged each month whether you use this image emailing system or not. The worst part, however, is that this monthly fee would apply to each and every scouting camera you run. Again, this real-time scouting concept is interesting, but it is, at the very least,

No matter what the scouting camera future holds, hunters will always aspire to see images like this!

ahead of its time. I, for one, am not ready to pay a monthly fee for each of my scouting cameras.

FUTURE FRONTIERS: WHAT ARE THE POSSIBILITIES?

When I was a youngster, one of the popular cartoons on television was the Jetsons. The Jetson family lived in space, in a space house, and drove around in space cars. That cartoon was popular in the 1970s. That is what futurists thought life after the turn of the century might be like. If you go back and look at the predictions that futurists made about today, the predictions are utterly ridiculous. We do not live in space and we do not drive around in space cars. We cannot even get past using gasoline to fuel our automobiles.

I remember one prediction that suggested, with the advent of the computer, that we would soon live in a paperless society. I do not know about you, but my desk is still covered with paper. In fact, believe it or not, I am writing this chapter longhand. Many of my chapters were written while in a treestand or ground blind. Once written, I will not input these words on my PC by typing them, but will use voice recognition software to read them into the computer. This voice recognition software was originally developed for those who do not have the physical capacity to type. Once it was developed, the developers, I suspect, decided that they could sell more of the software by also marketing it to hunt and peck typists like me. They were correct. But I still use paper.

My point is that it is futile to predict the future, as we do not know what emerging technologies may be ultimately applied to scouting cameras. History suggests that scouting cameras will continue to get better and better, with more and more user-friendly features, but that scouting cameras will not be reinvented like they were with the advent of digital technology. Time will tell. In the interim, enjoy your scouting cameras!

Index